A Woman Called Mary

Willi Ray

2nd Edition Published by Faith Books & MORE
ISBN 978-1-939761-37-8
(previously published by Purposeful Publishing and Media Services, Inc., ISBN 978-0-9831739-3-9)

Printed in the United States of America

This book is printed on acid-free paper.

3255 Lawrenceville-Suwanee Rd.
Suite P250
Suwanee, GA 30024
publishing@faithbooksandmore.com
faithbooksandmore.com

Ordering Information:
Quantity sales. Special discounts are available on quantity purchases by corporations, associations, and others. For details, contact the publisher at the address above.

Orders by U.S. trade bookstores and wholesalers. Please contact Ingram Book Company: Tel: (800) 937-8000; Email: orders@ingrambook.com or visit ipage.ingrambook.com.

Only the strong will survive, because God
is the author and finisher of our faith.
Hebrews 12:2 [NKJV]

Dedication

It is with great appreciation that we dedicate this book to our mother, Mary Dewalt and our beloved brother, Minister Lee A. Thomas. In addition, we dedicate this book to Pastor Elder Loren W. Burris; and to our children: Kalisha Reed, Sophia Johnson, Quiara Burris, Lamondez Thomas, Jerry Dewalt, Janevieair D. Ray, Dawanna A. Daniels, Lauren Burris, Aaronesha Brown, Lawrence Gibson Jr., Phillip Thomas, Damian Thomas, Kimon Reed Jr, Kaylin Reed, Razya Gibson, Brittany Thomas, Brianna Thomas, Rakesha Thomas, and Rickie Thomas Jr.

Our desire for A Woman Called Mary is that it will help guide you in difficult times. It was through the eyes of us all, Mary's children, that we realized the importance of our mother's legacy, a legacy which serves as a reminder of how hope never dies. Her legacy is the key to understanding how courage is the key to triumphant victories. When we needed a hero, A Woman Called Mary stepped forth. She is the wind beneath our wings. Mother, we all express how your loving service to your children is a job well done. Because of you, the apples on this family tree never fell far from the root.

All lessons learned, we have achieved most of the dreams we have set forth to conquer, because we know, love, and understand ourselves. Hug yourself mother, for that has been the best lesson you've ever taught your children.

Special thanks are in order for all my sisters and brothers for their participation. Lillie, Willie, Jean, Lisa, Marla, Dena, Myrtle, Velma, Rickie, and Lee; you guys are wonderful, and

I love you.

My prayer is for God to guide each of us into His perfect will with grace for the rest of our existence.

The Bible tells the story of Mary, the Mother of Jesus.
We felt the world would be suffering a great injustice if someone
did not tell the story of

A Woman Called Mary,
Mary Campbell Thomas Dewalt.

Table Of Contents

A Woman Called Mary
Introduction

The world would be at a great loss if someone did not tell the story of a woman called Mary, her struggle of courage, faith, love, and pain. A woman who it seemed effortlessly overcame many obstacles, and turned the world—the world her ten children knew—away from the South's bitter darkness. There she was, a woman standing proud, who displayed strong arms, death-defying will, and an immeasurable quantity of love and determination. With all supernatural powers and ordained anointment, the Lord bestowed upon her life the ability to transform the world her children lived in until it was a Sunday morning praise report in the making. This Woman Called Mary succeeded in showing how her love and determination to make a better life in a world that showed no mercy was an act only God could orchestrate. Mary just happened to be the instrument God wanted in His symphony.

Mary is an ancient name. It is a name which leaves a warm feeling in the heart and a smile in the soul. Mary is a name of great character and strength. It is a name of purity, innocence, great love, and powerful self-sacrifice. This brings me to my mother's name—Mary Campbell-Thomas-Dewalt. To the world, she is simply another woman named Mary, but to her ten children she is a hero, a hero who survived against all odds. She rose from the depths of despair to becoming a royal jewel in the eyes of all who saw her. She is A Woman Called Mary, and to quote a verse from the Bible "Her children grew up and called her blessed." (Prov. 31:28)

My name is Willie Benita Ray, and I am the second oldest daughter in the union of Johnny Thomas and Mary Campbell-Thomas-Dewalt. I am the narrator of our mother's story. Throughout this book, my siblings and I will introduce our stories and share bits and pieces of our lives shared with this woman we call Mary. We will also share some historical moments we all so clearly remember as if it was still the very day. The deaths of our maternal and paternal grandparents have left us knowing very little about our family tree. There are a few surviving family members on my maternal grandmother's side, but no survivors on our grandfather's side. We are hoping that someone will read this book and share with us vital information about our family's roots. This book is a part of our developing family tree.

If you have watched your beloved mother triumphantly cross all the hurdles in her life, then you will understand why we must tell the world about A Woman Called Mary.

Chapter 1
Getting Acquainted with Mary

Mary was born in Ruby, Mississippi on September 7, 1939 to Myrtle Stewart-Campbell and S. T. Campbell. They grew up poor in the south, a land of great hatreds, where the blood of the innocent flowed more often than water. S. T. worked as a hired hand, often traveling to seek work. Myrtle was a homemaker. Known to her five siblings as stubborn and self-minded, she did what she pleased, and always went against the grain. The thought of women being seen and not heard, especially in the South, charged Myrtle to reverse the process by being seen and heard. Folk all over town thought the white people were going to kill her if she kept losing mind of her place. Her family begged her not to talk back to white people, and not to look them in the eyes when they were talking to her. Myrtle was five feet, four inches tall, and had beautiful and fair skin tone, which the country folks called high-yeller. Myrtle viewed her fair skin being a pass, which granted her more rights than the darker colored folks.

Myrtle gave birth to a stillborn son in 1940. This misfortune placed severe strain on the marriage, because Myrtle knew S.T. wanted a son. Shortly thereafter Myrtle mustered the strength to try again for a second son. In 1942 Myrtle gave birth to a little girl. Soon after the birth of her daughter, Myrtle passed away. The cause of death was unknown. Due to the nature of times, white doctors never made house calls to black households, and the hospitals for blacks were too far away. Some thought it could have been a combination of excessive blood loss and complications during her labor; either way, something called for her life to end. Just when one thought S.T. could not handle anything else, one week later his baby girl passed away , off with the heavenly angels. This news shocked the town, and many people felt it was Myrtle coming back to take her child.

All of the bad luck in S.T.'s family had him pondering for a surefire escape plan from his sorrow. Sleep was something he daydreamed about, and whenever he found his way to his bed, it was not easy to escape it. Every day it became harder and harder to parent his daughter, he realized that he was not fit, mentally or physically, to raise his child. The pain of his broken heart triggered his cycle of deep mourning. Crying spells became his new talk. There was no closure because he never had the chance to say good-bye to his wife. Looking into Mary's eyes brought on a huge onset of memories, because she resembled her mother in many ways.

To deepen his depression, the marks his wife left inside the home reminded him of her every day. What was he going to do? In 1943 S.T. took the four-year-old child to his mother-in-law, Mary B. Steward, but grandmother Mary was too old to care for little Mary. Not able to remember what it was like to care for such a young child, her grandmother neglected to send little Mary to school until she was eight years old. Mary complained about the teasing done by other children about her height and age. Being older than her classmates, she felt awkward about being in class with kids who were still wetting their beds and their pants.

Mary's grandmother died the fall of 1949, and little Mary was propelled between heartache and pain again. Visited by the death angel once more, S.T.'s life revisited hell all over again. His mother-in-law was the bridge between heaven and hell for him; she helped him cope with life's disappointments, and now with her being gone, who was going to help him to cope? Still grieving over the death of a wife and two children, he felt compelled to question God, but words became much too heavy for his tongue to speak. No matter how much he tried to repent for every sin he committed, S.T. felt cursed, and he became upset by the thought of God hating him. In his heart he was sure everything he touched would die. With his mind wrapped around such a thought, he knew he had to get as far away from little Mary, or she too would die.

In thought of his late wife, he mourned at the loss of an undeveloped love affair. It was a love which died in the shadows of a fall day. Witnessing the death of love was like witnessing all the air being sucked out of the earth's atmosphere. "What good could possibly come from losing the one beautiful thing this world offered me?" he asked. "She was my glory and my one true love!" he said, with his shoulders slumped forward as if simulating the act of carrying heaven and earth on his rugged shoulders. Only God could feel this man's pain, a pain that was as deep and dark as any pit in hell. He wore his pain in such an unkempt fashion that his appearance changed. City folk said he was so empty that it may as well had been his ghost walking instead of him. To many, S.T. had already died. Grieving the death of a loved one ages a person and causes severe weight loss.

"Who is death that he has the right to rob a man of his one wee lamb, his air supply and sole reason for living? Who is death?" he shouted with clinched fists! Why Mary B., Lord? Why did you take her from us?

S.T. reflected back to when he took little three-year-old Mary to stay with his father-in-law, Solomon Steward, and his stepmother. They neglected and abused little Mary. Mary was often left alone and unsupervised. The lack of care proved to be unhealthy for Mary. One day S.T. arrived to find little Mary's feet bandaged. His stepmother explained how Mary saw her Grandpa putting hot coal into his boots to dry them out and she imitated him by putting hot coals into her boots. Not understanding that she needed to wait until the coals had cooled and been knocked out of the boots before putting them on, she placed her feet in the boots, and was marred with third degree burns to her feet.

Now with Mary B. gone, again S.T. was upset, and knew he had to find a home for his little girl. S.T. had to make a decision about where to home his daughter. He, too, was still trying to heal himself. He packed their bags and placed them beside the wall. His hands cradled his head tightly, hoping he could squeeze an idea out. He had to find a way to out-run the painful memories, for he was suffocating in the midst of this turmoil and despair. It seemed that being back in the town where his life fell apart was starting to tug on the strings of his heart. He felt a visit to his wife's and children's graves was in order. It had been five years since he last visit their graves.

As Mary walked circles around her father, he, on bended knee, cleared away the path to put flowers on the graves. Next thing he knew, he was talking to his wife. It was as if he was looking, speaking, and listening for some sort of heavenly guidance. "What should I do? Little Mary needs a mother figure in her life, and I cannot do this alone." In the midst of the leaves scraping the ground in the moisture-deprived heat, he waited for an answer from Myrtle.

"Daddy, mommy is always with me and you." Mary sung in such an innocent voice. Those words gave S.T. comfort for the moment. But the question of what to do with his baby girl remained unanswered.

The town folk said he was often heard talking about how his Myrtle called to him through the high wind which blew through the trees. His mind allowed him to believe that he could hear her singing from the kitchen or rocking on the porch. His heart just could not let go of the memories of his past life with Myrtle. Then one day, hastening with assurance about his next move, S.T. got up and started home.

Back at his stepmother's, S.T. grabbed their bags as he gave the place a once over, to make sure he was not leaving anything behind. He picked up his daughter, collected their belongings, and walked out without saying one single word.

Little Mary could tell something bad was about to happen by the way her father was breathing, mixed with the long pauses of silence. Nothing was ever more frightening to a child than being afraid of the dark. Passing miles of cornfields, Mary began to feel her father's pain and sorrow transfer into her spirit. Somehow, even as a small child, she learned to befriend her heartaches and pain. Mary's little eyes were searching for death or something worse over her father's long thin shoulders as they passed by rows and rows of cotton fields. Mary never said a word as she held her feelings in as best she could, while S.T. dragged his long torn legs down the dusty gravel road.

That hot August day Mary was amazed to feel tingling chills race through her small body. She looked up at the beautiful blue sky. She knew this sky; she knew it by many previous trips along this skyline, which lead to Aunt Lillie's house. With all the bad luck going on in her family, she wondered if Aunt Lillie was dead or sick. There had to be a reason for her father's long sad face and the visit to Aunt Lillie's house. As she looked beyond the cotton field and the trees, she noticed that the birds were still singing, and butterflies were dancing atop of beautiful flowers in the hot summer breeze. She smiled at the grasshoppers jumping back and forth as her father's foot pounded the ground. The heavens were undisturbed by whatever was upsetting her father. His heart was beating rapidly, and his grip around her waist was starting to loosen, as he walked past the hog playing in the mud hole along the side of Aunt Lillie's house.

S.T. stood at Aunt Lillie's door with his head lowered into his chest and his shoulders slumped. He could not find words to ask for help, or to explain why he stood there with his baby girl and a backpack, but the look on his pale, red face delivered the message. He was lost between this world and the agony of hell. He opened the screen door and put his daughter into the arms of Lillie without looking into her eyes to explain or say good-bye.

Aunt Lillie put Mary on the floor and reached for the backpack. S.T.'s tears dropped onto the top of Mary's head as he searched for the words which his paralyzed tongue just could not form; words needed to comfort his screaming daughter, who now understood what was happening, but his quivering lips failed to provide the comfort needed. Aunt Lillie held tightly to Mary, because she was struggling, screaming, and waving her arms back and forth, begging her father to take her back. Aunt Lille failed and could not hold the child any longer. Mary grabbed hold of her father, determined to leave with him. He peeled her razor sharp clenches from his legs as he stood there frozen. His daughter was screaming and begging him not to go, pleading for him to take her along. At that point, he wished he was dead. He picked little Mary up and held her tight, kissing her tear-stained face, and rubbing her back to comfort her.

For a moment little Mary was sure her desperate pleadings had persuaded her father to not leave her, but he placed her in Aunt Lillie's arms again. Aunt Lillie stepped back to prevent Little Mary from taking hold of her father again. Little Mary's head whipped around just in time to see S.T. tilt his head back to stop his runaway tears. Without asking any questions, Lillie found all the answers she needed to her questions smeared on his face. He reached out and patted Mary's head, and groaned in agony as he pulled away. Her tear stained face was like an image tattooed on his weeping heart. S.T. turned and slowly left the house.

His walk resembled a dead man's as he struggled down the hot dusty road, slowly putting one foot in front of the other one. His legs felt as if they weighed a ton, but his heart was even heavier. His heart was beating so fast that he thought it was going to come out through his mouth. He tightly pursed his red, chapped lips as he walked away. He could still hear his baby girl screaming for at least a mile down the hot country road, but he never looked back.

Once again Mary was brokenhearted and grief stricken, and in her eyes life was beyond unfair, because everyone she loved had left her.

Lillie Spates and her husband James, a man the town's people feared because he loved a good fistfight, raised Mary as best they could, but life in the South in those days was hard on everyone. Mary's life had started rough, so she never felt compelled to complain about the life she had with her Aunt Lillie. Surviving was not easy, and there never seemed to be enough food and money, but Mary always had a warm bed to sleep in. The Spates already had seven children to care for, and now this additional mouth to feed nearly pushed the family over the limit. Aunt Lillie bore seven children: Eddie, Rose Mae, James, Nig, Birdie B., Frank, and Joe Henry. Aunt Lillie did her best to make Mary comfortable.

Nonetheless, Mary always felt like an outsider, but there was nowhere else to go. She felt like she was intruding on her extended family, and although they took care of her, she still often cried in sadness, trying to find comfort. On many nights she cried herself to sleep, wondering where her father was. Mary dreamed about dancing with her mother in heaven, and in those dreams she would ask, "Mommy, why did you leave me?" With quivering lips and uncontrollable tears, more questions would follow. "Why did daddy stop being my daddy?" she would ask while rocking back and forth with her arms crossed. "Why didn't he take me with him?" she would yell out in frustration while her tears lapped beneath her chin. Pounding her fist into her pillow repeatedly, she would whisper in sadness, "Will I ever see you again?" "Why did God take both of you from me like that?" My granny is gone, and now I have no one who can love me like you all did." She buried her head in her pillow to conceal her moans. She cried until her eyes became sealed.

For two years little Mary frequently watched the same road that carried her father away, in hope that it would bring him back to her. Whenever she could, she would peer out the window, watching and waiting for him to return to her, but he never did. Every time she saw a stranger coming down the long dirt road she held her breath in anticipation, only to be disappointed when she saw that it wasn't him. But she never gave her hope away, and continued to believe that he would one day come back for her.

One day Aunt Lillie called Mary into the house. "Mary, you are eleven years old now, and it is time for you to face the truth that your father is never coming back. I am trying to stop you from setting yourself up for another big disappointment," she explained. Mary was confused and stunned for a second, then the life rushed back into her body. She wanted to cry, but refused to do so any more, for she was fresh out of tears. "Now I can stop worrying about him, because he didn't love me anyway. He forgot me," she said.

It broke Aunt Lillie's heart to hear so much pain planted in the heart of a child. She reached for Mary to hug her, but Mary pulled away. Instead, she walked out to find a quiet place to be alone with her pain and sorrow-filled thoughts.

Behind the house, deep into the field, she looked up at the sky with her fists gripped so tight that she stopped the circulation of blood in her hands. Now numb and full of fury, Mary's hands trembled as she yelled, "If it is tears you want God, I am fresh out! Love is just a word! I will never let anyone make me cry, ever again! I will never love anyone, and I will not use the word love! I hate that word, I hate it! It is a made-up word!" Surrounded by five foot tall sunflowers, she put her head in the palms of her hands and asked, "God, why didn't you let me die, too? Why am I alive? If this is living, being dead is better. At least I could be with my momma. Look at me God—just look at me. I am a little girl, but I have forgotten how to smile. Crying is all I know, and I am tired, I tell you! It's a big, old world, and I sit here all alone. That ain't fair, God!" Mary cried until she fell asleep in her Aunt's garden.

S.T. never wrote Mary any letters, or sent any word to her about himself; instead, he just vanished. Some folks said he moved to Chicago in the early 1950s and raised two twin boys with another woman. Others people said he disappeared without a trace.

Time passed, and Mary grew up sharing family chores and absorbing the household's Christian values. Her Aunt Lillie was a religious woman, and she introduced Mary to Jesus early in life. In retrospect, Mary often told us how she thanked God for her Aunt Lillie. She felt that Aunt Lillie did the best job she could in taking care of her. Aunt Lillie still made it evident from time to time, when stressed, that she still had her own husband and children to tend. Nonetheless, Mary came to value the strict upbringing and loads of good values Aunt Lille poured into her.

In the late fall, and in winter Mary went to school, but in the spring, summer, and early fall, to help supplement the family's income, she was in the fields picking cotton. She never was able to finish high school, because the fields always called for hands. Mary's dream of graduating from high school and finding a decent a job was stamped out by the reality of being born poor, black, and living in the Deep South.

Having no control or say over anything was both depressing and frightening. Mary watched the white children go to school throughout the school year, and play all summer long. She became well acquainted with the difference in the lifestyles of the black children and the white children. While her life revolved around picking and chopping cotton to help put food on the table, the white children were free to do as they pleased. Realizing the sad fact that she would never finish school, Mary dedicated herself to learning all she could during those winter days in the classroom.

Mary recalled that the talk of the town in May of 1954 had everyone in such a buzz. The Supreme Court outlawed school segregation in the Brown vs. Board of Education ruling. Mary was happy to hear how black people now had a better chance for quality education, but she wondered how that decision would affect black people in Mississippi, because white people punished any black persons who stepped out of line and tried to raise themselves above where the whites thought they belonged. She told us that the law stated that no segregation was allowed, but most black people lived in fear of their children going to school with violent white people. The state of Mississippi had its own way of doing things, and that didn't include any of the laws being revised to benefit the blacks. The state of Mississippi's goal was to keep all black people one step above being a slave. The freedom for a white to correct a black for stepping out of line was a freedom that should have ended with slavery.

Mary also recalled the brutal murder of Emmett Louis Till. "Such a shame that young boy had to die just for whistling at a young white woman," she would say. Sadly, Mr. Miles, owner of a general store, didn't like what young Emmett did. The two men who killed him were believed to be the owner and a worker from the store. Young Emmett was beaten severely, and his penis was cut off. The killers finally ended the torture by shooting Emmett, then dumping his body in the Tallahatchie River. In August of 1955, blacks in Glendora were outraged that an all-white jury found the two white killers innocent of the murder of Emmett Till. Life in Mississippi was hard, mean, and cold. Hardly ever was justice on the menu for serving to blacks in Mississippi. Mississippi was a racially motivated place that bred hatred. Blacks learned to live there and stay out of trouble with phrases such as, "Yes sir," "No sir," "Yes ma'am", and "No ma'am." Keeping one's head low and never looking a white person in the eyes was rewarded with survival.

Mother also talked quite often about what happened on December 1, 1955. That was the day Rosa Parks of Montgomery, Alabama showed great courage by refusing to give up her bus seat to a white man, as required by law. She described how black Americans held their breaths together, when they heard that Rosa Parks had openly defied the white man's law that she move to the back of the bus. Never mind that a vacant seat was awaiting her in the back, enough was enough. To the ears of a child, they all paid the same fare, so why did it matter where they sat?

Thinking back on the matter from the present day, we see now that white society was taking advantage of the system to calm its fear of blacks. Rules and laws to ensure continual racism and prejudiced behavior against black people spread faster than a home on fire. Mother said she was in her teens when the world exploded from the extreme and explosive demands black people made in regards to equal rights. Boycotting the buses was just another great moment added to the timeline of our people. It was a time of great pride and new hope, which united blacks across the nation.

Mom proudly talked about a young Baptist preacher who arrived on the scene with soul-stirring and spirit-lifting messages of hope, offering the nation healing. Sadly, I can remember my mother talking about how the healing did not come until later. Martin Luther King inspired black people to question the laws and demand freedom from an unjust society. My mother was mesmerized the first time she heard the Rev. King speak. A black man speaking so passionately, with strength and poise, with a hint of soul delivering tone, showed he was an educated man, taking a stand against the injustices black Americans faced.

Mother felt the words Dr. King spoke truly came from the lips of God. Dr. King's speeches and sermons struck at the core of some of the worst people who walked the earth. Dr. King was seen by many as the second, spiritual Moses, who had come to lead the children across the Red Sea of a troubled America. She said his nonviolent desegregation campaign was ingenious, and necessary for the time in which she lived. She said that while white people had their guns, dogs, water hoses, billy clubs, and unfair laws to control black people, they never expected black people to unite to resist their oppression.

Blacks formed their own unarmed armies, and during many marches demanded their civil rights. Dr. Martin Luther King had the ability to communicate with all types of people, both black and white. Dr. King was successful at getting many people to change their deeply rooted views on race. Mother said Dr. King had established a rapport with President John F. Kennedy and other high-ranking officials in government. He won the Nobel Peace Prize for his concept of achieving a better America. He turned America upside down with his ideals and his famous, "I Have a Dream" speech. Mother said she was happy to see Dr. King was a dark-skin man, because America was color-struck. She feared that only the light-skin blacks would have been given civil rights.

Mother often told us about all the black people who died, who gave their lives pursuing equality for us to get where we are now in America. She said we all should make the most of life and its privileges.

Mary felt lonely and lost within herself as she watched all the wonderful things happening around her. With all the pain Mary experienced, she wondered if there might be a yet unseen benefit in the rainbow for her to enjoy. Everyone wanted to see righteousness in all things. So it was sad to see all this greatness moving around her, and none of it touching her own life. Her days of looking for her father turned into days of looking for her Prince Charming.

In December 1956, at age 16, Mary fell in love with and

married Johnny Thomas, who was nick-named Music Man. He was a young musician who dreamed of the big time. He wanted to be a famous performer like B.B. King. He dreamed of following in Sonny Boy Williams' footsteps. He got gigs playing music and singing the blues in nightclubs and juke-houses on the weekends.

It is funny how black people enjoy singing about the things which make them sad, and feel despised as well about their own lives. Black people have sung about pain and wrong doing for so long that someone labeled their pains, calling them "the 'Blues". Mother lived in a day and time of great adversity and mistreatment, yet she did not hate. She said white people stole black artists' music, yet they lacked the ability to tap into the soul of the music. This music was born out of the heart and soul of everyday life, submerged in a communal type of pain, and swathed with a renaissance of unfathomable, cutting grief.

Although Johnny dreamed of being a major blues singer, he worked in the fields picking cotton, and switching into another role as an auto mechanic during the week, to feed the mouths in his family. September of 1957, their first child, a girl, was born. So fair-skin in color was the baby that the white midwife declared that she was white. Johnny began to question whether the child was his. Soon thereafter, baby Lillie's color began to darken to a beautiful, pink-tinted, light brown, almost beige-like color. This made both parents happy. Baby Lillie took her name after her Aunt Lillie.

A couple of years later Mary gave birth to her second girl, Willie Benita, who would be known as Willie B. She was born caramel-brown like her father, and Johnny accepted and received this baby much better than he did the first. She took name after his mother, Willie Bell Thomas. Johnny affectionately called his mother, "Bell," instead of "Momma." Johnny stated his reasoning for naming me Willie, saying that it was because I would be a strong and passionate woman. Funny, because I am just what my father said I would be.

During those days Johnny was getting more and more into his music, and was away from home more and more often as he traveled to perform. Because he needed more rehearsal time he gave up his job picking cotton. He had to prepare for his club acts. May of 1960, Mary gave birth to her third little girl in Minter City, Mississippi. My mother named her Mary Jean, because she was the third miracle of love, and a promise that she would never be alone again was offered through the special birth of this child. She was born light, bright, and almost white in color.

Blacks did not easily accept having a light-bright baby. The question of infidelity grew heavily, bringing a sense of shame and disgust upon the mother. The questioning of Mary's faithfulness was understandable to a certain degree, because Johnny's family was dark skin, and they refused to accept baby Mary Jean at one hundred percent. Mary Jean shared my mother's skin color. She was fair skin, and because of this my father's family did not like her much. It is so sad that, even today, in light of so much history, blacks still categorize one another based upon color.

Aunt Lillie paid a visit to mother sometime in 1960, delivering bad news. She had learned of the death of S.T. He had been killed during a robbery. Mary said she had given up on him for abandoning her, so it didn't hurt as much as it could have. The only reason why she shed tears was for missing the chance to see him one last time, just to say good-bye, or see you whenever. Finally, another chapter of another person suddenly leaving her life was closed. But Mary was excited and happy in her new universe of love and comfort. Moving from chapters of pain in her life, she embraced newness.

Living life on another avenue, Mary was excited because on April 1, 1962 various elements of the civil rights movement joined forces to launch a voter registration drive. In her residence of Glendora, Mississippi, blacks were being registered. Mother said she was about seven months pregnant at the time, but she wanted to witness her people showing up to register for their opportunity to vote. Mother said she was afraid to register herself because of the fear that riddled her soul. She remembered how Reverend George Lee of Belzoni, Mississippi had been killed in 1955. Rev. Lee was a preacher who used his pulpit and his printing press to urge blacks to vote. White officials disliked failing in their quest to end the Reverend's mission of voter registration. Once more, the white man's fear manifested itself in another evil plot, and one day Rev. Lee was ambushed while driving to his church. Shot numerous times, he staggered from his car, and died in route to the hospital.

Mother said that black people were extremely proud of Rev. Lee and the strength he displayed. She said the town's people felt loved and honored because Rev. Lee died fighting for their rights. In spite of their fear, black people continued the registration process, even if it meant their lives would be terminated. They had come too far to have their names removed from the registration list because of manmade fear. Mother always enlightened me with the way she spoke. She kept herself very current on politics and other events surrounding civil rights movement. I remember mother talking about Lamar Smith. On August 13, 1955, in Brookhaven Mississippi, Lamar Smith met his fate because of his determination to assist blacks to be able to take part in elections. So many blacks were losing their lives that it seemed someone died for each name added to the voter registration list. All through Mississippi, blacks were being killed, and the willingness of other blacks to testify about the murders decreased with the increase of threats. On the other hand, the white people didn't speak out, because they wanted to protect the white shooter.

The black people were hesitant to speak out because they knew justice in the heart of Mississippi was a stranger who only sparingly gave out miracles. In those days, Mississippi was sweltering with hate and the stench would last for many years. Yes, there were a few whites who really cared for and loved blacks as they did their own white sisters and brothers, but blacks were smart enough not to go looking for them. Who wanted to go searching for that needle in the haystack when finding it could be so painful?

In 1962, Mary gave birth to another beautiful daughter, Lisa Lee. Johnny fell in love again with another one of his little baby girls. Lisa was his perfect little princess. She had a full little fat face, and the cutest pucker lips. Her thick, curly hair looked like a wavy piece of carpet on her head. Johnny could not put her down; she slept on his shoulders most of the time. Her eyes were always searching the room for familiar faces. One thing about Lisa, she was always hungry. After done sucking her milk, she started sucking her fingers and anything that got close to her mouth. She smacked her little pink lips and started crying for more milk. As time grew on, so did Lisa's hearty appetite for food.

March of 1963, Mary gave birth to her fifth daughter, Marla. Wrapped in a beautiful copper color coat of brown skin, she was the only child born bald. My mother rocked her to sleep singing, "I got a baby name baldy Ma-Ronie." Marla cried all the time, and she craved her mother's attention.

When Marla was three months old, Medgar Evers, the director of the NAACP, was shot at his Jackson, Mississippi home by a sniper. At the time of his murder, his activities included leading a campaign for integration in Jackson. Mother said some people in high places wanted to stop the March on Washington. There was too much heat, and many people were wavering in the flames. There was a feeling of uncertainty in some people. Some wanted to cancel the March on Washington, but the soldiers of the Movement persevered. There were over 250,000 African Americans marching for civil rights in 1963.

My mother always connected her babies with historical events. She tossed her head back in disbelief as she spoke. "Marla was only six months old in September of 1963, when the story about the four little girls who died in the Sixteenth Street Baptist Church of Birmingham, Alabama came forth." I could still hear the tension in her voice as she spoke of how her heart went out to those little girls' mothers. She said, "I had five beautiful little girls and I couldn't imagine the pain those mothers were feeling."

Some evil soul had placed a bomb in the church, because the church had become a center for civil rights' meetings and marches. What cold-blooded devils they were! Why attack the spirit of a child? Adults can look their enemies in the eyes and receive a fair chance to fight on equal ground. Sadly, in the fight for civil rights, there has never been fairness, and there are no heroes, or Medals of Honor given in this war; just innocent casualties of black victims."

Mother's voice tone would change as she spoke. Full of knowledge, and long-suffering, she carried so many painful emotions for a long time. "How you fight a war unarmed when the enemy is carrying a gun? That fight was fixed and we were set up for failure in everything we did. We as black people have to out-think and out-maneuver the adversary with his own tricks. Violence never solved problems; it only compounded them."

Black people died for attempting to better themselves and their surrounding communities. No one fights forever without growing weary. My mother said that you couldn't hurt a man when he is willing to die for what he believes. She told us, "An army of evil men in the South, many of them part of the Ku Klux Klan, was in full power, and on a killing rampage. I've lost count of the number of black people killed in Mississippi between the 1940's and the 1960's." Mary spoke often about how America was not very good about keeping her promise of the pursuit of happiness. "America was built on the backs of blacks and innocent blood. The shame of it all is that the pursuit of happiness was discouraged by grown white, detestable men, if you can call them men, who dressed up in their own white bed sheets. They were proud enough to murder innocent people, but too cowardly to show their faces. Whom did they think they were fooling? The good Lord could see right through those hoods, and He is the one they will answer to for all the evil deeds they were doing."

My mother said that, to supplement the family's income, she went back to the fields to pick cotton. She left her five children with her in-laws Millia and Laura B. They quickly began to abusively mistreat three-year-old Mary Jean, beating her black and blue because they didn't like her lighter skin color. I heard my baby sister crying while being beaten, but not being much older than Mary Jean myself, there was little I could do to help her. Her screams pierced my heart. I pled with them to stop hitting my sister, and even tried to fight them off. I remember rocking my little sister to sleep as she cried. I lovingly nursed her bruises. They beat her because she reminded them of the white man's brutality against darker-skin black people. They beat her because of their own self-hatred. They beat her because they were defenseless against the life of poverty and the miserable existence they were forced to live.

Yes, they beat her for so many reasons, none of which had anything to do with my little sister. This was the first time I saw hatred on a black face against another black person. I learned to read the expression on white faces when they looked at black people. I learned early that skin color was as much of an issue with blacks as it was with whites. I hid Mary

Jean underneath the table and stood guard near the table to protect her until our mother got back from work to take us home. On that day I lost all respect for my daddy's side of the family. As I watched them from across the room, anger and chills raced through my body. At the age of four, I was filled with rage. I wanted to scream, but I didn't dare, in fear of what they would do to me. I wanted to hurt them beyond bad for what they did to my sister, but their size frightened me. I did all I could do, as my tears fell.

Then, my mother was knocking at the door, but no one wanted to answer it and let her in. The grown-ups began to leave the room when mother came in calling for me and my sisters to go home. Lillie was happy-go-lucky, and Lisa was dancing around mother's leg to be picked up. I looked at my little sister who was still underneath the table and asked her to come out so we could go home. When Mary Jean crawled out mother took one look at her and screamed out in anger, "What happened to my baby?" No one answered with truth, only lies. "She fell and hurt herself," one of them said. My mother remained silent as she examined Mary Jean's bruises. "She didn't fall and hurt herself—those mean ladies beat her up!" I shouted. "They kept hitting her and hitting her." I screamed out to free my emotions. My mother's eyes got teary and tight. Then she shouted words that I dared not repeat, and threatened to beat their behinds. I don't remember much more after that, but we were never left alone with them again.

As years passed, I kept the image of color and self-hatred in my head and my heart. I constantly asked questions about skin color. I later learned why dark-skin black people did not like the fair-skin blacks. Mother told me that, during the days of slavery, the lighter-skin slaves often worked inside the master's house, and were generally treated better than the darker-skin slaves, who usually toiled in the fields from sun up to sun down. The darker-skin slaves also far more frequently suffered brutal beatings, were burned alive, or lynched. Sometimes the lighter-skin blacks were permitted to discipline the darker-skin blacks. The darker-skin blacks were not permitted to learn to read or write, because it was illegal. Meanwhile, some of the lighter-skin slaves were granted the opportunity to read, write, and gain limited access to the finer things in life. Skin color played a big role in defining how far up or down darker-skin blacks stood on the food chain. This difference in treatment caused a great gulf between the darker-skin blacks and the fair-skin ones.

President Abraham Lincoln's Emancipation Proclamation had to be ratified by the 13th Amendment to free African Americans from slavery. But after that Black people continued to maintain the gulf between the lighter and the darker blacks.

During the 1920s black social clubs such as the Brown Bag Organization and the Blue Vein Society became popular. I am sure that were many more, but these were the ones we are familiar with. Both of these organizations barred darker-skin blacks from being members. The Brown Bag Organization members had to be lighter than a brown paper bag in order to become a member. The Blue Vein Society was an elitist group of middle class, lighter-skin blacks who believed they were superior to darker-skin blacks. If you wanted to be a member of the Blue Vein Society, then the wrist vein must be visible.

The lighter-skin blacks were labeled as mulatto. Mulattos were the group that occupied the middle territory between whites and dark-skin blacks. Discrimination from whites was a big problem, but discrimination from other blacks was in some ways an even bigger problem. Black discrimination against other blacks because of color is termed colorism. This term was coin by Alice Walker in 1982. Author of the book The Color Purple, she understood only too well the problem of color in the black race. I guess colorism is another jargon term used by America to classify black self-hatred behavior. This was simply a way of thinking passed down from the white slave masters, which somehow internalized itself at the core of our people's souls. I have to ask myself what better terminology should be used to define a cruel self-inflicted act of using mind games as a form of control of another human being.. Yes, we are still unable to heal mentally from the William Lynch inhumane method of "how to control your Niggers." If the Devil was called by a human name it would be "Willie Lynch." This man was liquid evil in the oceans of time.

Sometimes I think we need an exorcism to get rid of the separation-by-color demons unleashed by Willie Lynch. Believing that one color is superior to another one is wicked. Is the color red superior to white, black superior to orange, or is color just an adjective used to describe a noun? Unfortunately, colorism is the jargon, the poison the white masters fed the fair-skin blacks, and it attached itself to the bone marrow and the soul. Yes, hundreds of years later, and we still cannot uproot the demonic, poisonous color vines that run deep in some of our minds, bodies, and souls. The darker-skin people are fighting battles inside the black race as well as outside the black race.

I find it interesting to hear people say, "He or she is not black enough." What does that mean? Black enough for what? Who is doing the judging? We are either too black, or not black enough, when society wants to put us in our place, or remind us of that glass ceiling. I think they mean that attitude is not the criterion of what is acceptable to cross over into the mainstream of society. When society wants to close a door of opportunity, then they taunt us with "you are not black enough." We are all as black as we need to be as individuals; yes, we have all had the black experience. We as black people will never be free until we are free enough to be black regardless of the shade of our skin.

Mississippi, your bastard daughter has learned the lesson you were teaching on self-hatred years ago. Through the eyes of that little four-year-old girl, who saw her sister beaten for being born with fair skin, I now know what it all means. Black people are still separating themselves by skin color. Music videos feature black beauties who have passed the brown-bag test. I have not seen many dark-skin sisters in music videos. Most of the blacks who rise to the upper levels of Fortune 500 companies are fair-skin. Darker-skin blacks are still often having trouble finding jobs to establish themselves in life.

College sororities and fraternities will accept a fair-skin black person before a darker one. Spike Lee's movie School Daze brought the color problem between fair and dark skin, good and bad hair, front and center, so we each could examine our own attitudes and demons. Both black and white magazines look to fair skin to represent products and fashion. The lighter your skin, the easier it is for society to welcome you into its field of dreams.

If we cannot be black and free within our own race, then where do we darker-skin blacks find a safe haven to be black? Some lighter-skin blacks will never get the true picture of being oppressed, and the degradation most dark skin blacks lived through every day. Is there no value in black skin even for the people born with it? I have heard some blacks say, "I do not want to move in that neighborhood, because there are too many blacks there!" They would rather move into an area where they are not wanted and be treated with disrespect, just so they can brag about living next to white folk. I have this question—can America change its views on color? When will we as black people feel good about being black, and celebrate our blackness? Someone may respond with how "we are all black, and we are all proud," but to me, actions speak louder than words.

It was with overwhelming emotions that I watched America's first black president, who is of a lighter skin tone stand there with his dark skin, beautiful, well spoken, educated, accomplished wife, Michelle Obama, take the Oath of Office. As I sat and listened to President Obama's "Yes we can" slogan, I almost believed America was becoming color blind, and that the battle within the black race, and the long-lived race war between blacks and whites were soon to be things of the past. The future of America has a new face full of joy, and the pride of a nation has been elevated. If the slaves who built the White House knew that they were not only building a dwelling place for the master's white sons, but also for the future sons of black slaves and the Moors, who knows how it may have turned out. I am sure the Pyramids of Africa could not be compared to the architectural monument they would have built; unfortunately, the world will never know.

However, we are still in awe of Benjamin Banneker's work on the White House.

I sat there looking at my mother, seeing her eyes light up, and hearing the excitement in her voice as she said that never in her lifetime did she think she would see a black man as president. It soothed my soul. I watched her heart rise and fall with the every campaign battle Obama went through to get into the White House. My sixty-nine-year-old mother jumped up and down like a child on Christmas morning when it was announced that Obama had won the election, and would be the next President of the United States. As I watched her emotions soar to an all-time high, I asked myself, "Is this same type of emotion and hope she had during John F. Kennedy's presidency, was it the same as when Martin Luther King led the March on Washington, and during Bill Clinton's presidency?" Or was this emotion different? It felt different to me, watching her face light up like the noonday sun. I could see her breath a sigh of relief. As I sat there smiling, I wondered what else was locked behind those dark bluefish gray eyes, which had seen so much, as they gleamed like a beacon full of hope today. Can words express her heart-felt feelings about all of the history she lived through? So I asked the question, "Have we arrived, or are we merely learning how to survive?"

Again my mother smiled and said, "Never in my lifetime did I think I would live to see a black president." She then said, "You know, it is the old rats that cut the holes in the walls, and the mice run in and out the holes." As I pondered her words, she began to explain what that meant. Racism is in the hearts and the minds of older Americans, and the young are taught to enter and exit through that doorway. Then she smiled and said, "Thank God less holes are being cut in the walls today. Obama is President."

Before I could get this book finished, the shot that was heard around the world in 2012 reminded us that race is still an issue in America. A seventeen-year-old black boy, Trayvon Martin, who was "armed" with a bottle of iced tea and a deadly bag of skittles, was stalked, pursued, attacked, and murdered by George Zimmerman. Zimmerman racially profiled Martin, and left his truck to beat down and shoot the innocent boy, who was merely on his way home from a nearby store. The trial of George Zimmerman ended the same way as the one for the murderers of Emmett Till in 1955. Zimmerman was ruled to be "not guilty," and walked away from the trial before a non-black jury without punishment. We will always be reminded that the taking of a black life can be explained away by expert, credential-packing, liars, or by a pale-face lawyer who can convince the media and the jury that the iced tea and skittles carried by a hoodie-wearing young black boy on his way home was grounds for murder. Like my mother said, it is the old rats that cut the holes in the walls, and the young mice run in and out of them. The old rats have got to stop cutting holes into the walls. Why can they not sharpen their teeth on things that advance all of mankind? Here is food for thought—"love thy neighbor as thyself." That same little nine-year-old girl who witnessed racism at its worst during the 1960s is still devastated by the fact that the evil of racism is alive and well 40 years later. The question that comes to mind is, if Trayvon had been white and Zimmerman black, would the jury's verdict have been different? We as human beings can solve all kinds of mysteries, find cures for cancers, send a man to the moon, technologically advance the knowledge and the life of the world, but we cannot heal the demonic disease of racism? This epidemic of racism can be cured; but only love can cure disease of racism.

My mother stood up in church on August 15, 2014, the day after 18-year-old unarmed black teen Michael Brown was shot and killed in Ferguson, Missouri by an unjustified white policeman. She looked across the church at the black young men, and then said," I taught my boys how to live through police encounters. You young black boys need to have all your paper work in the car and ready to present at all times, answer the questions asked politely, and if possible do not run from the policemen. Life isn't always fair, but we need more of you all to live through the white attack on our black sons." She went on to say, "One day we will all find the freedom to live and be black in America. A black mother's sorrows begin when she gives birth to a black son, but God is in control."

One day my mother, thinking back on her life, said, "One of the worst fall seasons I can remember was November, 1963. This was the month that President John F. Kennedy was assassinated. Oh Lord, that was a day equal to the killing of King. Both men were great leaders." She told how his death was a great tragedy and loss to the black community. Black people were finally starting to believe it was possible for the world to change. Our people were building dreams and aiming high from the hope President John F Kennedy symbolized. His State of the Union Address promised hope for a new way of life. In our household, we respected John F. Kennedy, because he was an Irishman. At one time in history the Irish people were called awful names such as niggers and drunken rebels. They were classified as a race of people who would go nowhere. John F. Kennedy's father sent his son to the best schools to learn the ways of the European American. He carefully guided his son into politics, where he used his well-polished, smooth, handsome image to win the hearts of Americans. Society embraced him, but on the other side, some white Americans still had little respect for the Irish people. So, history repeats itself with Barack Obama as president and the lack of respect he endures.

I remember my mother taking the whole family down to our cousin June Spates' house to watch the news of Kennedy's death on his television. It was so sad. There was a great lost felt around the world by black people. Blacks felt as if the chance of a good life had been stolen when his life ended.

May of 1964 my mother gave birth to her sixth daughter. She named her Velma Jean. Velma was born dark skin, with a head full of thick black curly hair, and fat cheeks. I was not allowed to hold her, because I was considered too young, but my sister Lillie, who had become my mother's helper, held the baby a lot. The baby slept a lot, and was always smacking her lips and trying to put her entire fist in her mouth. Lillie was always bossing us around. Her favorite saying was, "Didn't I tell you not to do that again or I'll give you a spanking." I was mad at her and grew tired of hearing that. One day, I'll give you a spanking, I said to myself. My mother was constantly repeating, "Mind your sister!" Lillie was a little girl, but she was just a little too bossy. She had long, thick hair and a glowing shade of honey brown skin tone. Everyone called her the pretty one. They called me the middle child, so no one used my real name.

August of 1965 my mother gave birth to her seventh child, Myrtlesteen. There was something different about her birth. I heard the midwife and my mother say she was born with a veil over her face, and to them it meant trouble would follow her. I use to hear my mother praying late at night for Myrtle, asking God to bless and protect her from evil. I wanted to get a peek at the baby, to see if she was human, or a monster filled with evil.

I never understood what it all meant, but I remembered my first look at her. She was sweet and fat. Her toes were always sticking up in the air as she made cute baby sounds. I was happy that she was not a monster, as I once thought, although I still wanted to see the veil Myrtle was wearing when she was born. My mother breastfed all of her babies, and often complained that Myrtle was hard on her breast. Myrtle never slept at night, and I think she cried more than any other of the children except Marla. Now Marla had made crying a new language; I didn't think she would ever outgrow crying. My mother said Marla had colic a lot. I was happy when Myrtlesteen learned the difference between night and day, because the late night crying stopped.

Because my daddy was never home much, I felt I needed to protect my family, so I was the night guard. I was on watch 24 hours a day, seven days a week. The slightest noise would awaken me, and I often got up at night to make sure the doors were locked. Often times when I was awakened it was by my mother, who sat up late at night manually sewing dresses and nightgowns. My mother made the prettiest things by hand. I would spend hours sitting in one of those old wooden, straw bottom chairs, by the fireplace, watching mom cutting, trimming, and pulling the needle through the fabric. I was fascinated by her creativity. The last thought I would have on those nights was my desire to be just like my mother, making all my clothes by hand. The next morning I would come to, and find myself in my bed.

Getting all us children ready for bed was a long process. She would put three of us at once in the washtub. We had no running water inside the house, so she boiled big pots of water on the wood-burning stove and the gas stove in the kitchen while she brought in cold water, which she pumped from the well. She made about five or more trips to the pump filling the metal tub half way with cold water; then she added the hot water from the stoves until the water was just the right temperature. She would lift the smallest three children into the tub and scrub them squeaky clean. She would then take Marla, Velma, and Lisa out the tub, dry them with a towel, and rub them down with lotion and powder before dressing them in the cute pink warm gowns she made. After they brushed their teeth, they would stand in line to use the potty before going to bed. While the little ones were using the potty, mother was undressing the bigger three—Lillie, Mary Jean, and myself. After all that work, she repeated the process. After she bathed and dressed us, she would put us on our knees and guide us in our prayers. She then tucked us in and wished us a good night. There were two of us to a bed and we were not allowed to talk after the lights went out.

One night, I was awakened by mother's screams. She was frantically screaming about a fire in the house. I got up, put on my shoes, ran through the house to make sure everyone made it out safely. I held Mary Jean by the hand, and lead her out through the front door. I went back to check one more time to make sure no one was still in the house. Before I could get out the door two big hands grabbed me and carried me outside the house and into the yard where everyone had gathered. The hands that grabbed me belonged to our neighbor from down the road, who had come to help extinguish the fire.

The fire was hot, with blazing flames of yellow, orange, and red, mixed with streaks of blue. We were all outside watching the fire in deep snow. The snow was falling heavy that night, but we really did not focus on the snow because everything we owned was going up in smoke. More neighbors came running over to help put out the fire. My mother was busy counting us and calling our names. Mary Jean was missing! My mother screamed and called "Jean, Mary Jean." She realized that Mary Jean was still inside. People were trying to hold her back, but my mother broke free to run back inside the house for her baby girl. I was standing there shivering with fear watching and ready to run in there to get Jean if my mother had not gotten loose. My mother dodged the flames, ran in, and came out with Mary Jean, who had somehow managed to slip past everyone and go back inside and back to bed. Thankfully, the fire had not disturbed her room yet. The fire was burning a hole in the roof, and the windows were shattering due to the extreme heat.

I watched my mother risk her own life to save her child. We lost everything in the fire that snowy winter night. However, we realized how blessed we were to be alive and well even though we had lost our home and everything we owned. We stayed with friends and relatives for a while. It was an awful experience, because they treated us unkindly and had no shame in letting us know we were not welcome. I remember being mistreated by aunts, who called me "ugh-moe" and "the black one." My aunt pretended she could not remember my name, and this disturbed my mother greatly. My aunt constantly made comments to the effect that my mother should not have had all those children. My mother prayed a lot instead of quarrelling with them. She was forming a plan; but she was slow about letting the rest of us in on it.

My mother moved us all to Glendora, Mississippi. This city appeared to be populated people who were always shopping and partying, and it seemed to us children that the avenues were filled with candy stores. We moved next door to a woman named Mrs. Rat, who lived with her brother Jab. She was a big, round, fat woman with short, fat legs, and she always wore an apron. Mrs. Rat had strange looking eyes that always looked watery, as if they were made of glass. She baby-sat while mother was gone. She was nice; she baked us cookies, and often gave us ten pennies each. This was the first time a grownup liked all my sisters and me, and treated us kindly.

We never saw our father much. I guess he found that record deal he was looking for in the big city. He would come and visit every now and then, but that was only when his band had to sing in one of the local clubs. He showed up one day, and I did not know who he was. His hair was permed, slicked down on the sides and full on the top. He talked funny, dressed funny, and wore funny shoes. He called us over to him and hugged us, but as for me, I kept my distance. I was confused; this man did not look anything like my father.

Then he picked up his guitar and began to play and sing, and I became reassured by the sound of his voice. Yes, this stranger was my daddy! But the next morning like always, he had vanished.

Our father's being gone most of the time became the norm for us. His visits home happened less and less often, and finally just stopped altogether, leaving our mother to have to raise her children single-handed. Mary and Johnny's marriage did not legally end until he filed for divorce in 1977, and even then he didn't come to tell he was leaving for good; he mailed her the divorce papers. Mother's attitude was that we were not going to reach out to him. "If he wants to do something, he knows where we are," she told us. We learned later from one of his sisters that he went on to marry another woman and produce children with her.

February of 1967, mother gave birth to her last daughter, Dena. She was the prettiest baby I had ever seen. People used to come over to see Dena, who was a fat baby with a big, round, pie-shaped face and red skin tone. This was the first time I had ever seen baby bottles and disposable diapers. It was strange to see her sucking milk from a bottle, unlike the rest of us, who had been breast-fed. It seemed to me that using milk bottles was more difficult than breastfeeding, because my mother would have to get up in the middle of the night and be rattling pots to warm milk bottles while Dena's hungry screams tore through the house. My mother sang to calm the baby. The pot kept rattling in the middle of the night as February ended.

It was still cold outside, though I guess it was the end of

March, because the trees were blossoming. Time was passing, and it seemed that the baby (and the bottles of milk) was getting bigger, and the tone of the night screams for milk was now vibrato in nature. Nevertheless, however urgent the demands seemed, the bottle of warm milk always worked its magic. I told myself, while watching my mother leap to the floor night after night to answer the call of a screaming baby, that I would never have babies.

I watched my mother clean, cook, and work in the cotton fields as well as do odd jobs to put food on the table. We may not have been wealthy, but we always had food and a clean place to sleep. My mother struggled and prayed a lot, and God always made a way. Sometimes, if there was not enough food, my mother would not eat, but she would make sure we ate. This was a powerful example of love. Although mother never told us with words that she loved us, because she never heard those words when she grew up, we knew that she did. She knew how to show love; but there was no value in the word "love" for her. She did not want to cheapen her feelings for her children by telling us she loved us. In her heart, actions spoke louder than words.

My mother seemed to be okay, but her eyes were sad. Her eyes were always a mystery for me. The men would stand in line, tip their hats, and watch her walk down the street. They asked her out a lot, and she would say, "I don't have time for that. I have a family to tend to." I watched my mother walk, and I listened to the tone of her voice. I wondered if I would look like her when I grew up. It wasn't enough just being her daughter I wanted people to see her in me; I wanted to be like her.

My mother's Aunt Lillie always came to see us on Sundays. She wanted to make sure that my mother was sending us children to Sunday school. Even though my mother had not joined the church herself, she sent us to church every Sunday. Although we went to church every Sunday, we all felt alone, because most all of the other children had their parents with them. Some of the children had both parents there with them, and others were like us. We prayed that God would lead our mother into the church on a regular basis.

We learned a lot about hell and all the people who would be crying when the end of the world came. I remember wondering how could there be an ending of the world when I was still a child. I thought I was supposed to get old. None of it made any sense. Aunt Lillie gave us a picture of this white man who was a shepherd of sheep, and she called him Jesus. She told me to confess my sins to Jesus. Now, as I looked at the white man with the sheep I could not imagine why I would tell a white man my sins. I looked at Aunt Lillie and said, "No thanks, I'll keep my sins."

February of 1968, my mother gave birth to a son. She named him Rickie, and was so proud that, after having eight girls, a son was born. Little Rickie was a pale-skin, three-pound baby, born two months early. His lungs were undeveloped, and he had bronchitis. My mother had to place him in a glass tank called an incubator. One night my mother jumped up in a panic, because the house had gotten a little too cold. She was praying and putting coals in the big pot-bellied stove with the pipes that went up to the ceiling. I was up with her, of course. I had my nose plastered to the glass tank looking at my brother Rickie sleep. My mother kept telling to me come away from there and let the baby alone. I was curious as to why my mother was so afraid that cold winter night, I knew it had to do with this baby. She was breathing heavy, praying, and watching the thermostat as the temperature rose. I watched her lift little Rickie from his glass container and walk the floor covering him with more and more blankets and holding him tight against her bare chest. I watched her, but I didn't understand why this little boy kept her stressed, and awake all hours of the night. I just wanted her to go to sleep and sleep all night at least one night. It seems that ever since that little boy was born no one else could get any attention. I thought my mother had gotten mean after he was born. Little Rickie had to go to the hospital twice for bronchitis. As a result, the stress of not getting enough sleep was affecting my mother, and we found her yelling all the time for smallest things.

We couldn't play inside because we might wake the baby. Going in and out of the house was a no-no, because it might change the temperature in the house. We were constantly reminded that the baby needed to stay warm. I remember thinking who is this miserable baby boy who is causing us all to leave our happy lives behind just to make him happy? I didn't like that little boy; he looked like a little red rat, and he was too much trouble. I was too young to understand how delicate his little life was, and that he could have died at any given moment, but I was old enough to dislike him because of the problems he caused my mother and my sisters.

My little brother slept all night, and the house was quiet. Mother still rose up to feed him. I would, as usual, get up with her, because by now making sure everyone was safe, including Mother, was a part of my daily regimen.

On April 4, 1968, I thought the end of the world had come. I'd never seen so many black people walking the streets crying and screaming. The whole neighborhood was upset and crying. I was playing out back in a tree when I saw cars stopping in the middle of the dirt roads and people getting out their cars calling on God. The screaming echoed from miles away. I didn't know what happened. Was it really the end of the world? I wondered, because everyone was calling on the name of the Lord. I dropped whatever I had in my hands and ran home as fast as my legs could carry me. I was thinking that I had to find the picture with the sheep and white Jesus on it and quickly tell him my sins. My second thought was if this were the end of the world, I was sure my family would need me to protect them. I ran past my sisters, counting them as I went by. My mother was my main concern. I had to tell her that the end of the world was here, and help her get little Rickie ready to go meet the white Jesus with the sheep. I ran past my older sister Lillie, who had just come out of Mrs. Rat's house. Mrs. Rat had the only television in the neighborhood. Lillie was crying, and her face was red. I stopped in my tracks to see if she was okay, or was it that she didn't want to go to heaven to meet the white Jesus and the sheep. She told me that the end of the world had not come. The people were crying because Dr. Martin Luther King Jr. had been shot. She said he was dead. In my heart I thought it might as well be the end of the world now, because the white folk were on a mission to kill all the black people.

I remember wondering why anyone would kill a nice man like Dr. King. I went inside our house and found my mother looking out the window as she held little Rickie in her arms.

She was obviously upset, crying as she listened to the news on the radio. I walked in and stood there watching tears fall from her eyes. I could not find words to ask what was going to happen to black people now, but my body shook with tremendous fear, because our future was uncertain. Who will fight for our rights now, I wondered? At the tender age of nine years old, it felt like I was carrying the weight of the world on my shoulders. For the first time, I felt the burden of being black. In my own mind I felt paralyzed with fear and so many painful emotions. "Are the white people going to kill us as well? Will they sic the dogs on us, and burn crosses in our yards? Will they lynch us and hang us from a tree, or beat us with the same big black sticks I saw them whipping black people with on television?" My mind and my heart were racing a million miles a minute.

Every imaginable thought was running through my mind. I remember thinking that I was never going back to Mr. Walter's store again, because he was white. He owned the grocery store in Glendora, Mississippi, and he would stare at us with his nose turned up, and call my mother, "Gal." I slept little in those days. I hid the picture Aunt Lillie gave me of white Jesus with the sheep, because now this face represented fear and a race of mean people. In my mind and heart, the God I prayed to every night could not possibly be this white Jesus on the picture. I always told myself that God had to be a God of color to understand our way of life and watch over black people. Every time I heard a car pass or stop in the middle of the night, I jumped up and ran to the window to see if the white people had come to kill us. My mother knew I was having nightmares and crying in my sleep a lot, so one night she asked me what I was afraid of, and I told her that

I felt weak. I told her how I wanted to protect them from the evil white people. I didn't know how to fight so much hatred. On television, I saw the faces of the white people shouting mean words and throwing rocks, bricks, and bottles into crowds of black people. I saw police with night-sticks beating people who looked like us, and the blood coming from their heads and bodies. "Momma, how can I close my eyes to rest, when there are white people out there who want us dead? How can I sleep?" Momma said, "Go to sleep baby girl. God has his protective angels encamped around us." "Are these angels white?" I asked. "No, these angels look just like you and me," she whispered.

I got up and found the picture of white Jesus and the sheep. "Will Aunt Lillie get mad if I throw this picture away? Momma this man with the sheep looks like the same people who want to hurt black people. Please take it away; I am afraid of his face." My mother took it away with her and said that she would explain it to Aunt Lillie. I asked her not to leave yet, I wanted reassurance that the angels would keep us safe from the violent white people. "Momma, if the policemen are hurting black people without just cause, then who will help us?" The look on her face was one of questionable doubt, but yet and still she found words to reassure me to trust God to stand guard while I was sleeping. I went to sleep, but I could not understand why those people were so mean. They had everything and still were not happy. Why can't we all share this world? After all, it belongs to God and not us. That was my last thought before I went to sleep.

I awoke that next morning and found the family safe and happy and my mother still sitting on my bed. I wondered if she had been there all night. My mother told me that God wants us to love everyone, and not hate people just because of their skin color. I smiled at her and asked if anyone told the white people that. Again, she reminded me not to judge people by their skin color, and to take note on how good and bad existed in both races. She said, "God will take care of all the evil people." My mother smiled and said, "You can't live your life in fear of what other people might do. You owe it to yourself to be the best you can be in this life. Life has so many difficulties, and you have to learn to make the best out of what God gives you. Now get out of that bed and get ready for breakfast." When it came to telling the truth Mother did not waste time; she just said it.

I remember wondering how my mother knew so much about life. The expression on her face while she spoke was as if she had some deep insight about the future and the past. I kept her words tucked away in my heart. The look on mother's face made me realize that somewhere down the road the use of her encouragement would be needed in my own life. My mother sat us all down and explained to us that our skin color was going to make life a little hard to bear. A child's innocence is something to behold. I asked my mother if there is a better color to make life easier. My daddy's sisters didn't like light skin people, and white people didn't like black people. My thoughts were that there are too many people fussing over the color of a person's skin, and not enough people concerned about the welfare of the person in that particular skin color. We don't want to be picked on and despised just because we are black. Said Mother, "This is the only color you will ever be, but my dream is for each of my nine children to achieve great things despite the obstacles stacked against you. We are all we got. Everyone must take care of one another."

Then Mother told us about a big decision she had made. "I don't feel that I have given you all the best life that I can and, I am thinking of moving from Mississippi to the big city, East St. Louis, Illinois, because it is too hard making a living for nine children on my own. I've been struggling all my life and don't have much to show for it." She spoke softly, as a great layer of disappointment distorted her voice. She said that she refused to put us through a life of heartaches and disappointment like the one she had to live through. "My babies will have a better chance at the cloud with the silver lining in the city, because I am going to provide you all with the tools and atmosphere to achieve great things. I do not know how I am going to do this, but I am going to rescue my babies from poverty and a life of doom. You all mean the world to me, and I owe you all every good thing I can grab and hold to." I remembered hearing her voice, as it grew louder. Her eyes blankly stared out into open space. "My babies will have a chance. It may be hard and difficult, but we will make it, we will make it by the grace of God!" She prayed and asked God for courage, strength, and three angels to protect us on our trip. She pointed out that in the city there would be good doctors to help her take care of us better.

She said in the city we could complete two grades a year to make up for the grades we were behind in school because the school bus did not pick us up every day, and that we wouldn't have to walk miles to school. We used to miss school a lot, and that's how we got behind. It was as if we had attended school part-time. She told us that better housing opportunities, better jobs, and better schools awaited us in the city.

We all looked at each other and said nothing; we were confused about what life outside Mississippi would be like. Mississippi was all we knew, and we didn't think life outside of Mississippi would be for us. My mind wandered. I knew we didn't have a car, so how were we going to get to East St. Louis? One thing I knew for sure was that my mother's mind was made up, so that even though we didn't know how far away the city was, and did not have a car, we were leaving Mississippi. The death of Dr. Martin Luther King, Jr. had changed my mother somehow.

My mother got up early the next Monday morning, packed her bags, and adorned her size-eight figure with a dress. Her high yellow complexion, thick, brown, medium length hair all looked renewed that day. After nine children, her figure was still tight, and she was eye-rolling beautiful to look at. My mother's cousin, Birdie B., came to care for us for that week while my mother traveled to East St. Louis. Cousin Rosie Mae, who lived there, would help Momma find a house and sign up for welfare assistance.

Momma returned home with good news. She had a caseworker working on finding us a house. She got a job working to save money for the big trip to Illinois. However, all of her friends and family tried to sway her from raising her children in the city. They all felt that city life was not the life for a child. They had all kinds of concerns about a single woman with nine kids in the big city. Everyone we knew was at our house trying to talk mother out of leaving.

They told her she was crazy, and they tried to make her feel guilty by stating how a good mother would not take small children to a big dangerous city. Mother told them all that God would make a way and that she owes us a better life than Mississippi. She said she wanted her children to obtain a good education, to enable them to become someone. She looked forward to being proud of her babies.

At times, mother felt as if having a great life was a dream unfulfilled. She often wondered how different her life might have been under different circumstances. Mary explained to her friends and family that she didn't want her children to grow up not knowing about all the good things life had to offer. "Look at me," she said. "I am 27 years old, and I have nothing to show for my 27 years on this earth but my nine babies. I have a sixth grade education, and that is all I've gained in 27 years on God's green earth. That is not enough for my babies; this will never do for them. I don't care if some of you never speak to me again, or if you think I am making a terrible mistake, but what can be worse than the life we are living now?" Mary's friends and family told her they would not help her destroy her children's lives. After they all left, Mary prayed and asked God to bless her with the money for her trip. Mary felt God had already set his approval on their trip, because she didn't feel worried anymore. Peace settled itself in her heart and mind.

In the fall of 1968, mother packed our bags, and asked a neighbor to drive us to the bus station. While we were waiting for the bus, I could hear my mother praying to God asking him to place his protective angels all around us and to bless us with a safe trip. Mother, her nine children and three angels boarded the bus. Surely, Goodness and Mercy were the angels that followed us everywhere. Two hours and a million questions later, despite the noises of the bus, and the excitement of traveling through places we had never been, we fell asleep.

When we woke, mother had juices and sandwiches for us. We were all excited about the new life waiting for us in the city. My mother held little Rickie in her arms, and Lillie sat with my mother to help with the baby. I sat with the smaller children to watch over them. Just a few hours into the trip we began a continual chorus of, "Are we there yet?" The trip lasted nine full hours, and I believed my mother prayed the entire trip. All I remembered was whispers coming from her lips as she watched her sleeping children. I drifted off every now and then, but mostly I watched over my family. It seemed like that night lasted forever. We stared out into a darkness that was illuminated only when cars headlights shining passed in the night.

As time passed the sound of the bus' motor lulled us all to sleep again. When next we woke it was day, and the world looked so new! The thirteen of us climbed off the bus and stretched our legs. We looked around for anything that we could identify with, but there was nothing. There were no farm houses, no open fields of corn or cotton, no animals feeding in the pastures, no ponds of ducks, no forests to go gather wood from, nor any big flowing rivers to go fishing in. What was there were big, busy, beautiful, and crowded neighborhoods, and it seemed like everyone owned a car. People dressed differently, and they talked differently. Nevertheless, we settled in Illinois and began to adjust and learn to live in the city—all thirteen of us. Our three friends, Surely, Goodness, and Mercy settled in and became mother's eyes and ears. We loved having hot and cold running water and other necessities of living. Getting us ready for bed was easier for momma now. My mother enrolled in night school, but soon found it difficult to find a reliable sitter who would take good care of her children. She would come home and find homework undone and the children out of control. She quit night school because she needed to be at home to care for her children.

September of 1970, mother gave birth to her last child, and second son, Lee Arthur Thomas. My mother never remarried, because she didn't want a man living in our house with her girls. Up to that time Mother had regularly gone to local nightclubs with some of our aunts. She also enjoyed drinking wine and smoking cigarettes. She also liked to play cards and dance. She also dated some, but never brought any men home. Then Mother became a born again Christian in 1974, and both her and our lives changed even more. She renounced her sinful lifestyle, to live sanctified. No men, no more alcohol, and the bad language disappeared. Our lives became peaceful. Mother became both mother and father to us, without complaint. She didn't need a cape for us to see what a superwoman she came to be. Cooking hearty meals, cleaning house, caretaking, tutoring, and managing finances, she excelled in every aspect of motherhood. Whatever we needed, mother made sure we had it.

Having no room in her heart to raise lazy and unproductive women, mother taught all of her girls how to cook at the age of ten. In a tight rotation, each girl had to cook a meal from start to finish. We learned to cook from scratch; no shortcuts were allowed. We learned to cook everything, from fried chicken to baked ham, turkey and dressing, and varieties of desserts.

As for the chores, no one was exempt from doing laundry. Gosh, we hated that old style, wringer washer. Saturday was the day when nothing but laundry mattered. In order to execute this chore the way mother wanted, teamwork was necessary! One girl separated laundry and placed it inside the washer, two girls rinsed the clothes in three big metal tubs of water on the back porch, and two girls hung the laundry on the lines in the backyard. If any of us started to fuss and fight because someone failed in doing her share of work, more chores made their way onto her list.
We learned to work together, as long as my mother was in view. When mother was absent, we handled our disputes the way many siblings do! After finishing the laundry, we had to clean the entire house. Chores back then, compared to the chores of today, are very different! Children of today have no idea how to clean a house, unless their parents have stuck to the old school method. For us, there was no playtime, no anything, until the house was cared for. Mother didn't allow mess—PERIOD!

Cleaning house was like working a full-time job at the factory. We mopped the floors in every room, and washed the walls in the kitchen and the bathrooms. When the clothes were dry, we ironed them, folded them, and put them all away. My mother was a believer that hard work built great character. By the end of the day, when we all gathered to watch television, the television ended up watching us. Mother wanted us to be independent and smart young women. We all knew how to sew as well as groom ourselves. In my mother's eyes, there was no reason a young women should not know every essential about how to properly groom self. To her, presentation was everything.

Mother purchased a sewing machine to make our clothing. Already-made clothes in the stores was expensive, and I never saw money growing on the trees in our yard, so mother was smart, and decided to make all of our clothing. She was very skilled with her machine, so no matter where we traveled, we looked grand!

Mother was a strict disciplinarian. Sparing the rod and spoiling the child was a thought which never poisoned her mind. She raised a house full of well-mannered kids, I think, but I'll let my siblings share their views on this topic.

I remember one day when our youngest brother, Lee, who measured 6 foot 5 inches, was told to take out the trash. In crazed courage, he walked toward my mother and replied, "I'll take it out when I get ready." Mother hit him in his chest so quick and hard that he fell backwards in pain. After regaining herself, she said, "Now take that trash out!" Still dazed and confused as to what just occurred, Lee just laid there motionless in pain. My brother had thought his height had granted him some type of magical authority over my mother; he thought he could do what he wanted and not mind our mother. Now, at age 14, he learned the hard way that my mother was superwoman, and she had the strength to match. My mother is a superwoman, because she raised ten successful children. Nearly all of us have college degrees.

Mother made us want more out of life, instead of settling for things given.

Through this book I, with my sisters and brothers, want to inspire other families. Research your history, and establish your future. Become inspired by your grandmother's footsteps. See history from the road she traveled, and see the present, from the life she lived and the words she speaks. Last of all, I invite you to find your future with her courage and her strength in that world she will never see. Let her legacy be your guide to success.

Now I open the doors to my nine sisters and brothers to tell the world about this wonderful Woman called Mary. Our story will show you how strong her dedication in raising productive citizens of society was a sacrifice of undying love. Her focus was her children. Placing her life on pause, she denied herself the love of a man until we were grown. A strong woman understands the role of mother, and will do whatever it takes to make sure her children are cared for. Our mother is the epitome of strength, and for that, we love her.

PREPARE TO SEE HOW THIS WOMAN CALLED *MARY* SHAPED OUR LIVES!

Chapter 2
Lillie
Sister #1

I am the oldest of Mary's ten children. I will try to give my best in providing you with up-close and personal views of my mother. My mother is a private and shy woman, who, unfortunately, was bruised by the passing of time. I can testify that, in her weakness, strong love birthed itself. If I could, I would have cried her tears and borne her load, but the chance to do so never came my way, so my heartaches and my emotions swayed as I grew up in the shadow of this Woman Called Mary.

I am married to my soul mate of 26 years, Loren W. Burris, who is the pastor of Foundation of Truth Church of God In Christ. My mother is the president of the Mother's Board. We have three beautiful daughters. Our oldest daughter is Sophia Celeste Burris-Johnson. Her husband is Kenyon Johnson; they were married on November 15, 2003. Quiara Estyier Trinea, our second daughter, and Lauren Marie is the youngest. I was the first daughter on the scene. I have stood and have been blessed to see how Mary matured into a beautiful, glowing tower of strength.

Being the first-born child has its advantages and disadvantages. I was, for the most part, the obedient child. I think that, because my mother bonded with me first, she established a channel of trust and understanding. Early on I learned to identify with authority figures and grownup ideals. In my youth, I learned how to talk with people, and won the heart of any adult who loved children. Being self-confident and full of clever conversation, I succeed at improving my communication skills with adults. I competed for my mother's attention better than my siblings did. Other qualities that I have that I think came from being the first-born are being achievement-oriented, being obedient to rules, dependability, loyalty, and stubbornness. My mother often tells me that my ability to handle long-suffering humbled me. Around the time she shares her heart, she expressed her desire for me to make sound decisions about my life. She would say, "Be a strong woman, and deal with life accordingly, because life and its problems will not cease until you cease to be part of this earth." Through this testament of love, I felt my mother was trying to prevent me from dealing with issues she had dealt with in her life.

I remember growing up in Mississippi, where life was far from easy. In quest of an education, we took the daily bus ride to Black Bear School, where social grace was more important than schoolwork. During our kindergarten days, all of us kids were supposed to bring handkerchiefs to school, clean and pressed. If for some reason you forgot your handkerchief, trouble greeted you at the classroom door. The punishment in those days would be five swats with the paddle. The teachers cared more about the handkerchiefs than they did teaching.

They used the paddle in place of any real communication. You could be paddled at any given moment, without warning. The school my sister Willie and I went to was racist. The teacher would teach to everyone in the front rows, which is where the whites and the almost whites sat. The darker-skin kids sat in the back, and were mostly ignored by the teacher. With that lack of attention, the colored children suffered more if they failed to quickly grasp the lesson at hand. It was hard dealing with our mother when she learned that we failed to do our homework. "Where were you when the teacher was teaching? Why don't you know how to do your homework?" All the while, she helped us with our homework, and her fussing carried through the entire session. At that time we didn't know how to tell our mother that we were too black to be taught in class, and that our hands were ignored when we raised them to asked questions.

Finally, tired of us not knowing what to do with our homework, my mother took it upon herself to make a visit to the school, hoping to find out the problem. As my mother tried to enter the classroom, her entrance was barred, and she became upset. At that moment, my mother figured out what the problem was—we were on the dark side of the skin shade line.

Of course, with me being the oldest, I was responsible for my siblings. I am not complaining, because being the oldest made me develop a take-charge attitude when mom wasn't around. Order and sense of direction was necessary when momma wasn't around. All of my siblings loved me and thought of me as their second mother; all except my sister Willie. Willie was two hands full! She never paid mind to what I asked her to do. Mother would spend so much time threatening and punishing her when she failed to listen to me. I don't think it ever sunk into her head that I was in charge when my mother was not home. She had a mind of her own, and always did the opposite of what she was supposed to do. She knew that

I would give a full report when my mother returned, but she didn't care. Willie was spanked all the time. After her spankings, she would disappear for hours and not talk to a soul. Sometimes I think she enjoyed spankings. I didn't get too many spankings, because I did as I was told, and that made Willie angry. Yup, goody-two-shoes I was, and I wore them well. Willie wasn't a bad girl, but she just didn't like rules. The more spankings she got, the more stubborn she became. Thank God, my mother was able to straighten her out. She would talk to Willie until she was blue in the face. She was always trying to reason with her to be good and to open up and talk, but of course she wouldn't; she had a mind of her own. Sometimes I wondered if she would grow up and see adulthood.

Willie was a person of her word when it came to getting revenge. Once she told one of the kids in the neighborhood that she was going to get him back. Even if it took two months, she would do it! Mother tried to keep Willie in, to help avoid trouble, but that idea flew south. What happened was that one day this little boy, about Willie's age, threw a rock and hit her in the head. He was in his yard with two dogs when he did it. If not for those mean psycho dogs, Willie would have dealt with him accordingly right then and there. She yelled across the fence, "One day you won't have those dogs, and you got to come from behind that fence one of these days. I'll be waiting!" My mother put a bandage on her cut, and told her to stay in the house and let the boy alone. She told Willie that she would go talk to the little boy's mother.

Well, my mother talked to the boy's mother, but it flew far

from nice. "Tell your daughter to stop meddling, and maybe he won't have to throw rocks at her." My mother paused, collected herself, and calmly asked that the woman to keep her son alongside of her, and out of Willie's way. The woman laughed and said, "Like I said, you keep Willie away from him, and we won't have a problem. My son can take care of himself." My mother came home and told Willie to stay in the house for a while. A week later, mother forgot about keeping Willie indoors, and sent Willie and Lisa to the store. Willie was an eleven-year old girl, with a mean streak of tomboy within. As it happened, the boy was coming back from the store with a big bag of groceries, and from out of nowhere, Willie slapped the crap out of him, and the next thing we knew, groceries colored the pavement. With every blow Willie stuck to him, he tried to defend his pride, but the battle was soon to be lost. Poor boy, he got the beat-down of his life. He had two black eyes, a busted lip, a bloody nose, and a face full of scratches. Struck with rage, the boy's mother's came to pay my mother a visit, with her son in tow.

"Look what your daughter did to my son!"

"I am sorry, I'll talk to Willie." Not satisfied with my mother's answer, the woman was obviously looking for some type of deranged justice."

"Talking is not enough!" said the boy's mother.

"Well, I tried to talk to you about this earlier for a resolve, but it was clear that your way was the best way. Never mind what I cared about."

"I'm calling the police!" threatened the boy's mother.

And tell them what?" Mother questioned as she stood firm. "Oh, you mean tell them that your son started all of this by cracking my daughter in the head with a rock. I can tell them how hard I tried to resolve the situation before it got bad. At that moment Willie and Lisa walked up. Willie smiled at the boy and said, "I told you I would get you."

"She don't have a scratch on her, both of them must have jumped on my boy!" She asked her son, and he said, "It was her, momma, Willie did it!"

"I can't believe you let a girl beat you! Get your butt home and don't come out!" The woman yelled while slapping her son. For Willie, punishment was due because she failed to follow my mother's orders. My mother's hand was always full when it came to Willie.

Mary Jean was somewhat quiet, but always plotting some type adventure for the Three Musketeers to get into. Jean loved a good mystery; she lived for adventure and excitement. At the age of seven, she couldn't figure out how the telephone worked. She thought small people lived inside the telephone. She had watched too many episodes of The Land of the Giants. She took the telephone apart to free all the little people who lived in the telephone. By the time she took it apart and discovered that no one lived in the telephone, parts of it had fallen to the floor, and they looked like broken puzzle pieces. Once again, my mother had to pull out the rod of correction.

Mary Jean went through puberty at the same time I did, even though I was older by two-and-a-half years. She developed her womanly figure at an early age, and her figure was beautiful; the best in the neighborhood. We had to protect her from the older boys, because they thought she was older than she was. My mother never sent her anywhere alone, because she didn't want men chasing her. Poor Willie was so skinny; she looked like the letter "L" with a hump in the back. That's funny.

Jean loved to fight, and often got into trouble for fighting. Once, when they were thirteen and twelve, Willie and Jean got into this big fight. I tried to reason with them, but they were beyond reasoning. They fell through the front screen door and I moved back and allowed them go at it, because my mother was going to kill them, not me, when she got home. After the rumble, they realized they had broken the door. They quickly devised a plan to fix it. "Too late! I'm still telling," I remembered teasing them. Jean took the screwdriver and went down the street to an empty house, came back with a screen door, and put it on by herself. My mother whipped them both, for not respecting each other, and for using violence as a tool to solve their dispute.

They never fought again, at least not with each other. The both of them were relieved that mother did not promise them a whipping later, because that was torture. It was torture because if you are waiting on the whipping, your mind played all kinds of tricks, and tormented you three times worse than the whipping. My mother would say, "When I get you it will be for old and new!" At that point, you knew hell had no fury like the threat of Momma Mary. The thing you prayed to never hear was, "I am going to whip you like you stole the Good Lord's Supper!" Those words meant a serious beat-down. A good whipping was delivered for repeatedly disobeying her.

Lisa was timid and sweet. All she did was listen in on other people's conversations, and read other people's mail. She was the fourth-born and sometimes called the middle child. She would sit quietly for hours while I read to her, and then there were times where she would color pictures. Her appetite was so hardy it was hard to keep that child full. One day mother cooked a big pot of her favorite food, and allowed her to eat to her heart's content. She ate so much that her stomach looked like it was going to pop. If you did not get to the table in time, Lisa would eat both her food and yours, too! She was super skinny, so no one would ever guess that she could shovel food in her mouth like a grown man. After Lisa ate her dinner and everyone else's, she went to sleep.

Lisa had a problem distinguishing between reality and cartoons on television. She often played many practical jokes on her sisters. At times, her jokes left them in tears, and threatening to beat her down. She meant no harm, but she loved a good joke, and my mother had to show her the error of her ways. Once, Lisa hung a can of paint on a rope over the staircase, and rigged the steps so that when someone stepped on the trick step the can would swing down and hit them right in the face. Well, the trick was a success; it hit one of my little sisters in the face, and blood went everywhere. Lisa was devastated. She cried out, "Tom and Jerry never bled; no one was supposed to get hurt. It was a joke!" Lisa cried harder than the little one that was hit with the paint can. Luckily, the paint can was empty and the impact was not as severe as it could have been. I think she was sorry for what she had done, but even sorrier about what my mother was going to do to her. She was not allowed to pull any more practical jokes, and couldn't watch television for a long time.

She then became one of the Three Musketeers, and co-conspirators with Jean and Willie. They would sneak out of the house early in the morning and go looking for adventures in the neighborhood. They would come back before my mother woke up and tell wild stories about ghosts and the mole man. They had a gift for telling stories and using their imaginations. I never told my mother about this, but I pleaded with them to be careful and stay away from trouble.

Marla was a smart child at an early age. She wanted to hang with the Three Musketeers, but due to her small size, her sisters didn't want her around. She kept trying to force her way into the threesome, but always ended up in tears. I think she earned the name crybaby because she was always crying, for one reason or another. I can understand that, as the fifth child, she didn't fit in with the younger ones, and was too young for the older girls, so she struggled in finding her place. She excelled in school, always on the honor roll. She was the first product of the promise, which gave proof of where a good education could take you. I admired her strong will and determination to succeed; she loved reading romance books, and often talked about what her husband would be like when she grew up. Marla had a way of talking too much and getting into trouble, because she had a smart mouth. Jean and Lisa wore my mother down, which made it easy for Marla to get away with murder, but, of course, she never thought so.
The rest of the children were good and obedient to me. I love creating games and things, to keep them busy while my mother was gone. As head leader when my mother was not home, the power of the rod of correction fitted tightly in my hand.

My mother has always been a strong, courageous woman, one who could weather any storm. Being so strong, she inspired her daughters to fight through the storms in their own lives. Sometimes I think that it is hard for us to be passive wives, when our role model was always active. She gave us wisdom, knowledge, and understanding on how to survive with or without a man. She always told us, "You educate yourself, to be able to support yourself with or without a man." She would say, "A man is a want, not a necessity. You can live without some of your wants." My mother taught us to think for ourselves, and to stand up for our rights in the home and out in society.

My mother said, "Do your best to make your marriage work, give it your all, but without losing your identity as a woman and a mother. After you have given it your best and done all you can to make it work, peace lives with you. You should never go through life with regrets. Thinking about all the 'what if's' of life is a waste of time. A clear conscience comes after knowing you did all you could. First, love yourself, and find out what makes you happy, and don't give it up for anything. Secondly, keep your dreams and goals alive in your heart, and always work toward them as you grow." My mother advised us that once the children came, one's dreams are placed on hold (if they involved being away from home) until they are grown. My mother told me once, "Don't kill yourself trying to make that marriage work; put it in God's hands, and find a peaceful place to rest until He works it out." That was sound advice, and I stopped trying to work it out and gave it over to Jesus. Only He can do it better. My mother has always been there to advise her ten children on how to handle difficult problem. She has always given good advice based on the Bible and knowledge of the law. If she didn't have the answer, she would find out where to go get the information.

Having a sense of self is important to mother, and she taught us to believe in ourselves. She always spoke of how death would eventually come for us. It was just a part of the aging process. When you are old, that's when you'll reflect back on your life. That's when the heavy questions come. Questions such as, "How fulfilling was your life? Did you find the time to cultivate your dreams? Did you get to know the person inside?" Don't grow old with emptiness, she would tell us, it will leave you questioning if having a husband and children was enough. If it was, you will die happy, but if it wasn't, you will be filled with regret. "Somewhere in your lifetime, take some time to discover yourself and all the wonderful things God has wrapped inside you. Women too, were created to make sacrifices, along with giving and building lives for others."

I have always admired my mother, for she has been an inspiration to all of us. I saw my mother at both her best, and at her worst. I saw my mother go through changes when her marriage fell apart. Like any other woman, she was lost for a time, because marriages are supposed to last forever, yet hers failed. It wasn't what she did at this point that got my attention; it was what she did not do. She chose not to become lost in her grief. She did not want her children to feel forgotten, for she knew we all depended upon her greatly. She cried, but was not complacent, because her survivor instincts led her to fight, and to rise above the pain. Sometimes days and weeks would go by without a smile on her face, but her silent courage was always visible. Sometimes she would keep busy just to keep from crying and falling apart. She cried when she thought we were asleep, but I heard her pray for strength and direction, and for food to feed her children.

I could see that she was troubled, but not perplexed. Never once did she show any sign of regret for being a single parent. We didn't lose one day of love from our mother. Her love was fresh and new every day, like the mercies of God. I realized that my mother truly loved us, and only death could separate her from us. She vowed never to be lonely again, and to always have love shouldering her. We surrounded her like flowers at the base of a tree.

As long as I can remember, she has always lived as an independent, hardworking, and caring person. Once, I must have been about four years old, I remember my mother trying to prepare dinner for my sisters and me. My sisters were crying because they were hungry. She would walk back and forth comforting us, in the midst of all the chaos. The little ones were following her and crying and she patiently kept cooking and comforting them. They drove me crazy that fall night. In my eyes, my mother's real first name was Saint.

Mother is the best cook ever. She loved cooking fried chicken, rice, green beans, and big, fluffy homemade biscuits. When the food was ready, she would pray over it and fix the little ones' plates first, and sit the plates near an open window to cool, while she fixed the rest of our plates. We had a wood-burning stove in the middle room, which warmed the whole house. While the children were eating, she would continue throwing more wood in the stove, to get the house a certain temperature to begin the bathing process.

This was a long, drawn-out process, bringing water in from the outside well and heating it on the stove. After everyone bathed, she would pull out her sewing machine and finished clothing projects. The last thing I remember her doing is making sure that everyone had clean clothes to put on the next day. She would iron the clothes, and place them in a pile on a chair in the middle room.

I thank my mother for a strict spiritual upbringing. She taught us to respect our elders, stay out of grown folks' conversations, and say "Yes, Ma'am" or "No, Sir." She instructed us to respect ourselves and others around us. "Don't get caught in a closed, questionable place with boys. Say no to premarital sex. Find out if a boy is pursuing you for your mind, or for your body. Dress appropriately, to prevent others from disrespecting you. Tell the truth, even if you will be punished for it. Pull your pants up, and put a belt on. Work for what you want!"

Not only did she care about her own children, she encouraged all of the teenagers in the neighborhood to get summer jobs through CETA [the Comprehensive Employment Training Act] to buy the things that some parents couldn't afford. We learned early about the difference between needs and wants! The values of yesterday are lost in today's society. Parents today have more to contend with in raising a child. Parents today have to compete with the media and the latest trends in fashion, while trying to teach their children good values.

Today's society tells our young girls to expose their breasts even before they are developed, and to pull their skirts way above their thighs until their bottoms are exposed, for only then will they feel loved. "Talk dirty and flirt with the world to get what you want," says society. "Use your body, wear revealing clothing, and shake everything when you walk, and the world will roll out the red carpet. Don't wait on hard work to get what you want; sleep your way up the ladder, while staying high on drugs (to prevent your conscience from catching up with reality).

My mother would have killed us for some of the things that children today think are normal and acceptable. Raised to be respectable young women, there was a whole host of mannerisms we learned. The behaviors of dressing, talking, and walking like ladies, were an everyday part of our life, not just an act. I felt we were the most hated girls in every neighborhood we lived in, because of the high standards my mother had for us. We were called "stuck-up!" Mom made sure we steered away from socializing with the bad girls of the neighborhood. I didn't like her strictness then, but I so appreciate it now!

We played with each other. We didn't need playmates from the neighborhood; we had each other. We had fun entertaining each other, because there was always a list of endless games we could play without becoming bored. I think the greatest blessing in the world is a large family, one filled with love and respect for each other. Loneliness never crept into our home. We were always there for each other; we always shared secrets and dreams.

The average age for dating in the house was 17, at least for me. Mother put the boys through the third degree, until the idea of never coming back, along with stopping all contact with us at school, was the only solution left. I think my mother enjoyed interrogating the guys. I'm sure she was dying from laughter on the inside. Sitting there with a dead-pan face on, she would ask the guy, "What is your folks' name? Where do you live? How long have you lived there? What is your GPA? What do your parents do for a living? What are your hobbies? Do you date a lot? Why are you interested in my daughter? Have you ever been in trouble with the police? Do you make it a habit of skipping school? What time do your parents expect you home? Do they know where you are now?"

I loved how she would give me two dimes, and remind me to call her if the guy forgot his manners. She taught us at an early age the importance of being treated like Queens. After her interrogations, we would leave the house, but all the boys seemed to be afraid thereafter, they walked the straightest line possible. If there was something questionable about the date night, she would ask us about it. Innocence and creativity had to be transparent in our answers. This woman was so strict! I was sure she was scanning our bodies with her fierce eyes, looking for the boys' fingerprints. Thank God, my dates wore gloves (just kidding)! We were brainwashed by my mother's famous quote, "You don't until you say I do!" She trusted me, and I didn't want to lose her trust. Having my mother's trust meant everything to me, and I never wanted to lose it.

Mother had a way of making each one of us feel as if we were her favorite. She had a special relationship with each one of us. She would listen and talk to me as if I was the only one on earth. My mother combed and styled my hair during our conversations. She would show me how to fix the latest hairstyles, as well as how to coordinate my wardrobe. Fashion was our favorite conversation piece. When she was with my sister Willie, they would sew and make clothes, and talk for hours. They would go shopping for patterns and design new outfits. When she was with my sister Jean, they would talk about her boredom, and how to challenge her into creating better ways to use her time effectively. Helping her think about her future was something my mother discussed with her on a regular basis. When with Lisa, the topic was boys. The rules relating to boys were the highlight of their talks. When she was with Marla, they would talk about who was picking on her, and why they were bothering her. Marla would go on and on about her philosophy on life and religion. Mother, smiling, would talk to her, and listen to her points. Her talk about trying to grow up too fast with Marla played over many times. She would calm Marla's spirit by praising her good behavior, and rejoicing in her level of intelligence. In the end, Marla felt her mother's love, and left with a smile. Funny thing, that girl would be there next week for the same conversation! Ha!

Talking with Velma was all about building her confidence, as well as helping her find her voice. She wanted her to be able to stand up for herself when the time presented itself. "Be a good girl" was the message mother had for Myrtlesteen. "And stop taking other people things!" She felt that her queries of life, and led her into the fast lane. While some children learn from their parents' warnings, others learned from their experiences.

Dena and mother would talk about the importance of school, as well as stopping her from being a crybaby. Dena would draw pictures and mother would display them as if they were fine pieces of art. Even discussions as to why Dena was so afraid of getting her hair washed were hilarious. We still don't know why that girl ran when she saw mother coming with a bottle of shampoo. My brother Rickie would come home preaching every sermon he heard from church. My mother enjoyed it. She always told him what a fine preacher he would make one day. Lee was all about using his hands. She noticed how good he was with his hands and always told him how great he would be making things.

My mother had a way of making everyone feel special, and of spending time with all the children. I don't know how she did it, but she made mothering look easy. Now that I am a mother, I know it's not as easy as it looks. So much praying and sleepless nights were on her to-do list.

My mother raised ten of us by herself. At one point, people looked down on us because we were being raised without a father. Sometimes they tried to make us feel bad about coming from a single-parent home. We all wondered how it would feel to experience an upbringing in a two-parent home. Mother said if there is a father in the home that is wonderful, but if not, the mother has the responsibility to be both mother and father.

The parent in the home has to instill good values, and raise their children to be productive citizens. Teach them about family, relationship roles, education, and religious values. My mother did all of that, and much more. It may sound as if I am writing a woman-of-the-year nomination for my mother, but a crown and a dozen roses would not do her justice. She deserves praise for her honor, her courage, her faith, her unselfish love, and never-tiring words of encouragement. She is the best mother and father. Words cannot describe the feelings my heart contains for my mother. She is a God-sent blessing to all of us. In retrospect, I cry when I think of her struggles and her triumphs. When God made mother, a new mold was created. I am still in awe and amazement of her wisdom, knowledge, and understanding about life and her ten children.

I smile every time I reach for a telephone to call her. She enjoys listening to me talk about all the things that matters in my life, and I so enjoy telling her. I do not think my mother could ever get tired of listening to me talk about my day, the children, my husband, the church, and all the things I find pleasure in. I admire my mother more than any living being. As you see, this book shows the power of A Woman Called Mary.

Chapter 3
Willie Ray
Sister #2

The first thing I want people to know about me is that, because of my mother, I have a BA in Health Care Administration and an MBA in Business. Without my mother heavily influencing the importance of education in my mind, I would not be the woman I am today.

I grew up in the late 70s and 80s. It was a time of plaids, checkers, blow-out hairstyles, and basement house parties. I don't know why I mentioned the house parties, because I never went to one, but that was a big thing in those days. Teenaged boys referred to their conversations with the ladies as "rap." A guy would say, "Hey beautiful, you are too fine not to be mine, can we rap for a little?" Young girls were not supposed to resist a guy with a strong rap, so to speak. The Jackson 5 was the hottest group in the world, and Michael Jackson was the one to watch. Tina Turner, The Pointer Sisters, Donna Summers, Olivia Newton-John, Peaches and Herb, The Isley Brothers, The Temptations, Parliament Funkadelic, and The O'Jays made the music teenagers grooved to. I grew up slow, while my sisters rushed along.

Things were changing all around me, and I did not adjust to change well. I wanted things to slow down until I was ready to change, but that wasn't the way life worked. Time waits on no man; we are all slaves to Father Time. My teenage years were weird because I grew up in church. I watched the world revolve around the church. My mother didn't let us date until we were seventeen. All the other girls were going out experiencing their first kisses, their first dates, their first slow dances, and their first romances, while I was busy experiencing my first altar-call. I was saved in 1975, at the age of 14, and my heart was dedicated to serving God. During this time, I was very involved with learning how to love myself. There was a period where I hated myself and it took me nine years to look at myself in the mirror with love. All the mean names my aunts called me while growing up, and the secret I hid in my soul, had eaten its way through my self-image, and I became blind to my own beauty.

I admire my mother Mary for many beautiful reasons. She was the light in my world of darkness. She had (and still has) a rare type of courage. Do you know how much courage it takes for a single mother of ten children to raise successful adults? Her definition for courage believes that "Faith is the substance of things hope for, and the evidence of things not seen," to quote the Bible. She was a living example that it took courage to have faith, and faith without the courage to believe was dead.

Some people believe you can live without faith and courage, but those who believe that have never lived in a world hidden in the mysteries of time. All that means is that no one can see down the road until you get there, and that is why one must live by faith. She could have aborted us, or placed us up for adoption, but courage led her in the right direction. I'm sure her bold decision to follow through on raising her children didn't come without headaches and sleepless nights. Society teaches that the norm is for young women to make it easy on themselves by killing unwanted babies, or place them up for adoption, and go on with their lives. But doing either of these things would have provided no advantage for my mother. I truly believe we were a necessity in our mother's life.

Somewhere in Mary's life, she needed to prove that success was possible, even when you started at the bottom. Mother taught us to weather the storms of life, and to look for the positive aspect in the rainbow. She helped me through many difficult times in my life. If it wasn't for my mother's love and prayers, I would have been dead by now. I am sure I owe her my life, and so much more. She gave me the strength to look in the mirror and love the child the glass reflected into my eyes. She gave me the courage to believe in myself, to dream aloud, and to have a new and beautiful attitude about life. Through her love, I am made whole.

I am not going to tell anyone that life was always easy for the ten of us, because it wasn't. One thing I will tell everyone is that God was good to us, and that our three friends—Surely, Goodness, and Mercy—helped us out in tight spaces.

My mother has always been a praying woman, and when she didn't know what to do, she prayed, and God answered her prayers. We went to church so much that we all vowed to stop going when we grew up, to take a vacation from church, so to speak. We got burned out on church-going, but were never crazy enough to abandon our faith, or the Lord. Through church, mother shaped and molded us. The Ten Commandments created our value system, and our personalities took form.

The Bible speaks of raising up a child in the way that he should go and when he is old, it will not depart from him. Everything that went on in church we were a part of. We may have left the body of the church, but the body of Christ was always in our heart. We knew the importance of having Christ in our lives. One by one, we all came back, because we needed that personal walk with Jesus. Mother taught us how to live holy and walk uprightly before God. Mother raised us by herself, and she did a wonderful job. No matter how difficult it was, she was determined to do it right.

We complained all the time, because mother was strict and determined to raising decent human beings. My sisters Mary Jean and Lisa wanted to go to parties and school dances, but my mother's answer was always "no." One Friday evening Lisa and Jean were determined to go to the school dance. There was a tree outside of our two-story home that hung over our bedroom window. I and two of my sisters shared a large room on the second floor of our house. With its various curves and corners, it felt like three different rooms. The girls' plan was to sneak out the window, climb down the big tree that stood beside the house, and go to the dance. I was afraid to climb down that tree and go with them, but I was a less daring type than those two. They waited to leave once mother fell asleep. Mother would come to the top of the steps and say good night, and she wouldn't move until she heard us all say goodnight in return. That night, the plan was for me to say goodnight for Jean and Lisa.

The two dropped their clothes down to the ground in a plastic bag, and climbed down the big tree to get dressed. I prayed for them to make it back home safely. Mother was restless that night. I heard her up in the middle of the night checking the doors and windows. I came down stairs to see if she suspected something was wrong. She heard me coming down the steps and started calling out names. "It's Willie, mom," I said.

"Why aren't you sleeping?" she asked.

"I heard you down here," I said. She was up praying and reading her Bible. I sat and talked with her until I became sleepy, then went upstairs to see if Jean and Lisa were back. I had a feeling that my mother knew something was wrong, but just didn't know what. They sneaked back in somewhere between five and six in the morning. My mother got us all up at eight for our usual Saturday chores of washing and cleaning. Lisa and Jean were tired and dragging, but were unable to get any rest at all, because mother would add more work to what they already had to do for the day. Every time they tried to relax or sit down, she made them get up and do more work. After all the cleaning, washing, ironing, and cooking, those two had to cut the grass. They cut the grass in tears, but they did it. Until this day, they wonder if my mother knew that they sneaked out that night. They didn't get to bed to sleep until 6:00 o'clock that evening. It was a long time before they sneaked out the window again! The next time they wanted to go to some event, they asked and pleaded like the rest of us.

My mother was always a strong woman. The first time I saw her breakdown was December of 1978. It was a cold day outside, and snow was on the ground. It was the early part of December because we had not yet celebrated Christmas. Mother woke us up early that morning. She stood at the bottom of the stairs shouting, "Willie B., Jean, Lisa, Marla, all of you come down here!" She stood us all in a row in the living room, and looked us up and down. The expression on her face was one I failed to identify with. I was afraid to ask what was wrong, just in case it was me who was in big trouble. I waited like the rest of us for her to speak. We stood there confused and worried for a good five minutes. They felt like an eternity. Then she sat on the couch in front of us, and then sprang back to her feet and cleared her throat. We all held our breath as she began to speak.

"Somebody here is pregnant," she said. Shocked and scared, we remained silent. "God showed me in a dream that someone is pregnant." I knew my mother was off her rocker at that point. She didn't let any boys come over, and if they did, she made them so uncomfortable with all those questions that they chose to never come back.

I smiled and said, "I am not pregnant; I am still a virgin, unfortunately." My mother's expression proved that my "joke" was not funny. Her forehead became cluttered with weird shaped wrinkles, and her lips tightened and her left eye dropped, then she looked me straight in the eyes. I cleared my throat and shut my mouth so nothing could fall out of it.

"Who is it!" she asked?

"Not me!" we all sung aloud.

"Get out of here, Marla. I know it is not you. I am taking you three to the doctor," she said.

"Fine," I said, "but I still won't be pregnant." Lisa did not say anything; she just looked surprised. Then Jean yelled out, "It's me, I am pregnant." Lisa and I were shocked, because we thought my mother was for some reason giving us a scare, but it was true. Lisa and I looked at Jean and took one large step back, leaving Jean on the front line to face my mother's wrath alone.

My mother looked at Jean, and pain rushed across her face. She lost about two shades of color. She sat in the chair and put her head in her hands. She cried like a baby. It is a painful thing to watch your mother cry aloud. Lisa and I were still frozen in our tracks. We could not move, we both were glued to the living room floor one step behind Jean. We never saw our mother cry. We didn't know what to do. About a million thoughts and emotions were trying to process inside my head. Strong as mother is, I didn't know she could cry. This was all new, and seeing her in a helpless state hurt more than anything.

Lisa freed herself from the floor and walked slowly up the stairs. I was trying to figure out what to say to my mother to ease her pain. I had so many questions for Jean but right now, I was angry and disappointed with her. How could she do this to us, and why didn't she use something? My mother stopped crying and then asked, "How far along are you, Jean?" "Three months..."
"How did it happen?" my mother asked?
"I skipped school." Jean said. "I'm sorry, I didn't know I could get pregnant on the first time. I am so sorry this happened."
"With whom did this happen?" mother asked.
"Bruce," she said, as she wiped the tears away. Bruce was a cousin to our next-door neighbors. I didn't even know they

liked each other. That whole day was quiet, and no one spoke. It was as if someone in the family had died. We all fell into instant depression, and no one was hungry but the little ones.

My mother called Bruce's parents, and told them that Jean was pregnant. She requested a meeting to discuss the situation. Mother told Jean that she will do school first, then be a mother to her child afterwards. Fun time was over! Jean said that she got pregnant because she listened to her sex education teacher, who had said that the rhythm method was effective in preventing pregnancy. Jean confused the day you ovulate with the days that you could not get pregnant. Mother was upset that Jean was taking a class that she never authorized. Mother went up to the school to find out why she had not been informed that Jean had been skipping school. The schoolteacher and the principal explained to my mother that the notes she sent for Jean to miss school was due to her being sick. Jean never thought about the consequences, and now the whole family was hurting. I watched my mother's meek expressions at church while the other members were whispering about us. My mother said she raised us all the best that she knew how, and thought she was on top of things. She said that Jean was never late coming home from school, and that her grades remained in good standing, so she had no reason to suspect that something like this was going on. As time flew by, Jean got bigger and bigger. The pressure from her peers talking about her caused her to dance with ideas about dropping out of school. Soon, Jean realized that she was not the only one being talked about. She learned that the whole family's name was being dragged through the town's dirt. We all learned that no one lives this life without making mistakes.

When the time came, Jean gave birth to a beautiful little girl. My mother kept teaching and guiding Jean into motherhood. What started out to be a nightmare became a blessing. My mother ignored the whispering and gossiping of the neighbors. Mother and all of us loved Jean through it all. Her love for Jean allowed her to rise above the pain and disappointment and to meet Jean's needs. I watched my mother ease into her new role of grandmother with a smile.

My mother would not give up on Jean, even though Jean wanted to give up on herself. Her unplanned pregnancy forced her grow up fast, and made her miss the enjoyment of being a teen. It seems that Jean had been trying to find her teenage life for 25 years. My mother is still the driving force in Jean's life. She is the reason that Jean kept trying, no matter what was going on.

My mother became a stronger wall of protection for all of her children. She educated us on the subject of life, as well as how to get up when you've been knocked down. Trusting God for guidance when the hard times came would get us through, she taught us.

I watched in amazement as I witnessed my mother being pulled in so many different directions, yet she remained intact. We all wanted her to support us in whatever we were doing. Her counsel was something we always sought after. She taught us the importance on making sound, not rash, decisions. "Always pray before you make a move. Put God first in all you do."

One day recently, I asked my mother when her happiest time

in life was, and she said, "The present." She explained that it was because all of her children were grown. She thanked God for blessing her children with good health, and having never seeing the inside walls of a prison or jail. She said that last part jokingly, but I knew that she was seriously glad that none of us have gotten into trouble with the Law. All of us have good jobs and careers. Most of us have college degrees or some form of career training. She thanks God for all the beautiful grandchildren.

My mother lived in this small house that none of her children liked, but to her it was heaven. The house represented a place in time, none of us understood, nor could we separate mother from it. It is the time and space that she exhaled, because all the children were grown and on their own. This is where she found solitude in her own life. We offered to buy her a better home, but she says there were too many memories in this one to leave, and she takes pride in how she has fixed up the house with her own hands. Yes, she rebuilt that house herself. She did not want us to go in debt for her. "I'm doing just fine." She kindly stated.

We spoil her rotten on her birthdays, and on Mother's Day. Those two holidays are special because we can spoil her without restraint. When the hands that rock the cradle are as loving and caring as hers, the world is a better place. There is an old African saying, "It takes a village to raise one child." That is great truth in that quote, but in America it seems that no one is concerned about your children but you. Everyone is afraid to say anything to other folk's children. Times have changed. You have to depend on God and personal knowledge to raise your own children. A good Biblical quote is, "Except God watches the house, the watchman watches in vain." A mother cannot be everywhere at the same time. I still wonder how she managed to know what we were doing, and how she managed to show up just in time—only God knows. We thought she really had eyes in the back of her head!

I had my first boyfriend during 12th grade. I learned from him that I was beautiful. He said that boys never approached me because they didn't know how to approach me. Because of what happened at the tender age of five, I saw myself through the eyes of pain and shame, but now I was learning to see myself through the eyes of love. The first relationship was short-lived. My mother and my religious values took their toll on that relationship. My mother would not let me go anywhere with him, because he had his own car and she didn't trust that element. He was always trying to tempt me into sneaking and do things that were not part of my beliefs. I was forced to choose between him and my religious faith; therefore I chose God.

My high school prom was hard to swallow. My mother allowed me to go only with the boy of her choice. While I'm sitting with this so-called choirboy my mother had picked out from church, I had to watch my now ex-boyfriend with some other girl make out on the dance floor all night. My time to be home was midnight, and I was glad because it meant that I did not have to sit and watch him and his girlfriend make out all night. I remembered my mother's last words were, "Don't let me have to come looking for you." I remember getting home, taking off that big heavy blue dress and sitting on the roof with the warm air caressing my body.

I questioned my judgment about my religion and boys. Was I afraid of boys, or was it the feeling of falling in love that scared me? I thank God for giving me the strength to stand up under the peer pressure of what I thought was love. I have to admit—my heart was broken, but saving myself for marriage was the right thing to do. Mother said the best gift to give to your husband is your virginity.

After time passed along, I felt as if it was my time to move. Dating was an activity I now partook in. I remember the look on my mother's face one night when my boyfriend Gerald and I returned home from a date. She looked at Gerald and said, "How dare you walk in my house like that." I froze in my tracks and said,
"Like what?"
"What have you two been doing?" she asked? "Nothing, I brought her back in the same condition she left." He cautiously stated, not knowing what the problem was.
"I hope you two know what happens with all that kissing." We looked at each other and said, "Yes ma'am."

"Gerald, the next time you walk in my house in that condition put your hands in your pockets." We both looked down at his pants. He was so embarrassed. He apologized and left quickly. I started patting the back of my neck as if it was on fire. At that moment, my greatest fear was losing my mother's trust. My mother's trust meant everything to me. Tears layered the corners of my eyes. I was disappointed; I didn't know a simple kiss could cause an embarrassing situation like that for a boy.

My mother came to my room and explained that she realized all of the feelings I was experiencing. She made sure that

I understood the definition of caution, and allowing room for the devil to move in should not be allowed. She didn't believe I would deliberately do wrong, but dating was a dangerous game. With dating came a sense of commitment and responsibility on so many adult levels.

I married Gerald A. Ray, on 16 July 1983. Five years later I gave birth to our daughter, Janevieair. She was a beautiful little girl, full of the power of God. But after eight years of marriage, I began to go through a metamorphic-like phase. One morning I woke up, and it felt as if the greatness of my life had been stolen. There was a huge void in my life. I wanted more, but more of what? I had a good husband, and a beautiful daughter, so why wasn't I happy? We both were Christians, and had a full life that revolved around the church. Yet I felt empty. My soul thirsted for a cold satisfying drink of life. I had been good for so long that I felt as if I was missing out on something. I had grown up in church and had saved myself for marriage, and truthfully, I had no time to roam.

Feeling as such, did not mean I wanted to live a life of sin, but just having the chance to experiment could have saved me from some of my hardships. I lived my life by the book, I followed all the rules, and I was still not happy. I searched my soul through and through for what was missing. Depression was not the issue, or was it? A desire for more, for better, never left me. Another round of self-exploration was due. In the end, it was all about finding Willi Ray.

I talked to my mother, and she said that sometimes a woman has to develop her dreams. She said that a woman has ambitions too, and sometime a woman can balance a career, a family, and her dreams. She also said, "Please keep the lines of communication open with your husband." Some men do not understand a woman's search for self. I was afraid to dream because they would never fit in my religious lifestyle, now those dreams have come to haunt me. My body ached inside for the dreams I never lived. I am not foolish; I know some dreams were never meant to be, but what about the dreams of destiny? My mother told me that God has a calling on my life and there are things he wants me to do and that is the reason I am so restless. I looked for the cure for my restless in all the wrong places.

My marriage fell apart because my husband didn't understand that I needed more. I started taking voice lessons, and my sessions of soul searching frustrated him greatly. In his heart, he felt as if he failed at making me happy. That wasn't the case. From there, he started hanging out all night and the marriage crumbled like a sand castle in the rain. We separated, and I was heartbroken, because my marriage was meant to be forever. Mother was there for me, and when I thought I couldn't go on, she pushed me further. When I cried, she dried my tears and reminded me of how God can bear my heaviest burden.

"Willie, this too shall pass, lean on God and your mother." Her words were comforting to my soul. I never saw a woman so strong and so full of knowledge. She told me I wasn't the only woman in the world with a failed marriage.

I lived through it, and guess what; life is on the other side. "Whether the two of you work it out or not, you will survive," mother reminded me. I did not have the patience to wait on my husband so I gave up on him and God. I was mad at the both of them, I was mad at God because I felt He had the power to fix the marriage; but He turned away. I was mad at Gerald because he was selfish and expected me to wait until he was ready to come home.

I backslid from the church and began my journey of both good and evil. I called it good and evil because this was the time I began to try to recoup "lost time" from being raised in the church. I was brainwashed into believing that I had missed fun and excitement.

"Girl, come and go with me to this; it won't hurt to get out." That was one of the many lines that lured me to the streets. I was also taught how to dress for the streets. I put on the low-cut, short dresses, push-up bras, and high-heeled shoes. When I put those kinds of clothes on, my soul grieved my spirit. I felt as if I had shot someone. I felt God's heartbreak as I stepped out on the scene looking for the greener pastures. I had turned my back on God and all he had done for me, looking for a "good time." I went to the club, and my sister taught me how to drink and how to act. My soul was vexed and my heart moaned, but I pushed passed. I had to know what people of the world were chasing so hard that they were willing to go to hell for it. I wanted to taste a glass of cold wine and sway the night away to a love song. I wanted to see how it felt to club all night. I wanted to see what I had missed while growing up in church.

I could still hear the voice of God call every time I was alone, but I foolishly ignored it. The same voice I had learned to listen to and obey for over twenty years was one

I now wanted to drown out. I was going downhill and the brakes were missing. Sometimes I cried when I failed to feel the presence of God. The life I knew was as empty as an abandoned building. I had lost the two things that meant the world to me, God and Gerald.

Modeling was a dream I wanted to pursue. I went to a modeling agency, and they loved me. The acceptance from people gave me courage. My walk changed and I was now a part of the beautiful people. I wanted to feel beautiful again. The beauty I felt in church was of the spirit; this beauty was of the flesh. I began to wear makeup to hide the ugliness contained within. The people loved me. They said I had an air of innocence about myself. As quiet as it was kept, what they saw as an air of innocence was the Spirit of God in me.

I was traveling out of town every weekend, modeling and going to parties, but I still felt empty inside. When the drugs were sat before me, it was as if I could literally hear my mother praying. "Lord save my child, and keep her safe from all hurt, harm, and danger." God did not let me touch the drugs. I had men with big dollars pulling at me to be their arm-candy for public functions. They were sending limos and money, but I could hear my mother praying, "Lord, save my baby." The devil was constantly whispering dirty lies, saying things like, "A girl like you can have the world at your beck and call."

The most amazing thing about my mother is she was one woman, with one heart, who yet managed to love all ten of her wonderful and different children. I must admit, there were times where we all accused her of loving the other child more. We were all jealous, and never wanted to share her with the other siblings. She always assured us that her love would not run out, and that there was plenty of it to go around. We still teased each other about stealing too much time, or for being too needy. The truth is, her love was strong, wide, and long, and though sometimes thin, she still covered the ten of us like a white fitted sheet.

The thing I didn't understand as a child, but understand now as an adult, is her never using the word love. To my mother that word had lost it savor, and was empty of truth. She never told us that she loved us. The word "love" was rarely used in our family because, as a child, the word love, meant nothing but broken promises to mother. Mother grew up with a false conception of what love really meant. To her that word would best serve humanity if it was never used. To her, it's a word which builds you up only to let you be swallowed by the hard falls of life. It is a word muttered to her by her dying mother. This was afterwards followed by years of loneliness and unbridled heartaches. It was a last word cried to her by her father, right before he walked down that long dirty road in Mississippi, never to return. Her husband used this same cruel word before he walked away and never came back. She never used that word to us, but she always showed love. In her heart action speaks louder than words.

Which is more important, you may ask? Is it better to grow up with the word love as a comfort mat, and believe it when it's used? Some will fight to the grave saying that you must tell a child that you love them in order for the child to grow up secure in life. We are all well, secure, and normal because of the love we were shown by our mother, even though she didn't say, "I love you."
One of the main things I love the most about my mother is

her ability to change our perception of the world in which we live. We were poor, but mother made us feel rich. We were indeed a rich family. We were all each other had, and my mother made sure we understood how to show love, and to respect each other. She made sure we found comfort and joy in each other. Our joy gave us courage to lean on each other in difficult times. This was a perfect support system for us all. As each of us grew up and became more independent, we all still remain connected to our life force, each other.

The most miraculous thing about mother is how she had a limited education, but she taught us great people skills. My mother has always expressed to us how important it is to stand tall, and look people in the eyes, and honestly express your intentions. My mother also informed us about how being black meant that your ability to communicate well was either a blessing or a curse; it just depended on how others felt about you, as well as their selves. Mother taught us to speak proper English as well as she knew how. She taught us to speak from the heart. She said, "Choose your words carefully, because you may only get one time to tell your story." My mother is so wonderful to talk to, because she speaks with wisdom. When she speaks, it is as if she has seen the future, because it always comes to pass.

Among her words of wisdom are, "In the corporate world, expect to be challenged. Expect to be picked out, to be picked on, because this system was not designed for you. Count it all joy when your professionalism is tested, because it will only make you stronger and even more determined."

In closing, I would tell the world that she is something special.

She may not have understood all the heartaches and pain that brought her here today, but it was the very same pains and disappointments that shaped her character to become a wall of towering strength for her ten children. I just want to say sincerely, I love her very much. It was because of this Woman Called Mary that I found the true meaning of love.

Mother, because of you, I love myself, and I carefully used the word love, because you have redeemed it back to its natural state in my lifetime. I hope that one day you can stand up in front of a room full of people and tell each of your children, "I love you."

We know that you love us, but by saying these words, "I love you," we will know that time has healed all those old battle scars. In my eyes, Mother, there is one more battle to fight. Though you are mature in the arena of life, you are still a soldier in the battle of life. The enemy that robbed you of so many precious moments in time will never die until you behead the beast.

So fight this last war and redeem the word love in your own heart and soul. We will then rejoice with you because then, and only then, will you truly be free.

Mother, you have fought a good fight of life, and we salute you, The Woman Called Mary.

Chapter 4
Mary Jean
Sister #3

I am Mary Jean, but Jean suits me fine. I am the third child of Mary Dewalt. I have two daughters, Kalishia La'shaunda Thomas, and Aaroneshia. They are my pride and joy. Kalishia has a son, Kemon, and a baby boy, Kaylin. I am a proud mother and grandmother.

I am going to talk to you about my wonderful mother, The Woman Called Mary. Before you can understand how my mother affected my life, you have to learn about Jean. I am a product of my mother's love. Before you can see her as the person I proclaim to be heaven-sent into this world, see me as her greatest inspiration of love.

I am not perfect, by a long shot. Like many of you, I am curious about life. I did not know how good I had it at home until I grew up. I complained about everything, and wanted to be free to walk outside of my mother's shadow. My mother cast a long shadow, with powerful consequences. I was as fine as wine, and everyone told me that all the time. My mother expected me to keep all this beauty hid away from the world, no not me. I tried to share her ideals about life, and I even respected her and her values, but I had to be me. I was born bored about everything. I might have been too bored to cry when the doctor spanked my bottom at birth. I am like Eve in the Garden of Eden; if the tree of the knowledge of good and evil is in front of me, I am going to go for it, and take my punishment later. I wanted to live and take chances. I wanted to explore time and events. I don't want to die empty and then go to hell. If am going to hell, then I am going in limo style.

The church people are always preaching about hell. Do not get me wrong; I believe that hell exists, but man was given a free will to choose, and I am walking the path I have chosen in life. I am not a bad girl; I just like to have fun. Sometimes I think fun had a hold on me. No matter what was happening in my life I always took good care of business and my family.

When I grew up in the late '70s and '80s, my mother tried to keep me grounded in the church. The call of the wild was louder than the whispers of God, and I answered that call. I thought that I had been sheltered far too long, and I had to break free. Maybe getting pregnant wasn't the best way to declare my independence from my mother, but it opened my eyes. It made me grow up fast, and learn about the consequences of my actions. My mother was right about waiting to be sexually active until you are grown or married, but she was sanctified. Such persons are supposed to abstain from sex. I was a saved and sanctified Christian for at least two years, so I lived that life. "You cannot wear pants, you cannot drink, nor go to dances, you can't wear makeup, you must not use bad words, and you certainly cannot have premarital sex." Well, there were too many negatives or can't dos for me. There was not enough excitement in it, but I admire anyone who can live that way. I needed to take some risks, take some chances. For a while, I was too green to hang out with the world, so I had to learn to fit in. I tried things that I knew were wrong but so did most people, but that was all in growing up . I had to find people who wanted to party and live a little. I am not crazy, I knew the level of depth I wanted to test the water in. The funny thing is where ever I went I could not out run the voice of God and God's love. Like my sisters we all grew us and left church but God called us back one by one.

When trouble came in like a flood, my mother constantly let me know that I could make it. She gave me courage to fight to get on the other side of my midnights. She prayed without ceasing, and she anointed me with oil. Thank God, she never gave up on me. Sometimes I think she slept on the floor at the front door of my heart when she wasn't watching over me. She got me through troubled times with love. I didn't have to worry about my business being all over the neighborhood, my mother kept my secrets. My mother is wonderful. She is an angel of mercy on my lowest days. She pointed out so many blessing that God had given me. She reminded me that my children needed their mother, so be the book that they can read.

She would always start by saying, "I raised you better than this Jean. I am not going to let you destroy yourself like this. You don't need this kind of environment around your children." Now this is no reflection on her, or how she raised me, I just wanted to live my own life. It may not be the life she would have chosen for me, but it is my life.

Maybe I am still being rebellious from the teenage life I never had. I had my first daughter at the age of eighteen, and I lost something that year. I was kicked into full bloom motherhood while my other sisters were dating and growing up. I wanted the freedom to live the carefree life of a teenager, but all that was taken from me. I have been searching for those years ever since. Maybe you can't go back in time, but for twenty years I have been making up for losing those years. I party like there is no tomorrow, and I come home when I get ready. I might drink a little, but never will I get drunk. I only smoke cigarettes, and stay away from drugs. I still can't find that place in time I lost because I was in a hurry to grow up.

What I would tell young people today is, "Take your time and enjoy life. Sex does not prove that you love him or that he loves you. So what is the rush? Hang out with your girlfriends, do fun things, talk to your mother before having sex. Sex is not all it's cracked up to be, and the price is too high to experiment with it."

If I had talked to my mother beforehand, I am sure she would rather have given me pills versus my giving her a granddaughter. My mother helps me deal with the difficult times in my life. She made me stay in school and get my high school diploma. She said, "You made one mistake, and I am not going to let you wallow in it. It is not the end of the world; just know that your life will drastically change.

My mother is so amazing to me. She is my best friend. We share a wonderful closeness, rooted in respect, and bound by love. I can't imagine where I would be if anyone else would have been my mother. She loved me enough to stand by me right or wrong. Thank God, she kept me in her prayers, and believed in me until I was strong enough to believe in myself. She gave enough love to the rebellious storm inside of me to calm the storm.

No matter how bad I was, she never stopped loving me. Truthfully, I felt her love the hardest when I struggled. Even when I did not want to hear about how God spared my life, and that He loved me, she was there to remind me of my blessings. Mother still makes unannounced house calls and nosey phone calls, because she loves me.

There were times I felt she loved me less because I kept her on her knees, so much. I am a mom and I know about late night prayer on my knees asking God to bless my children. One thing my mother taught us is how to pray. God and I met when I was saved as a teenager and I know how to reach heaven when I need help.   Nevertheless, because of her prayers, I was able to grow in grace and mercy. I have a good job with a good company. God blessed me to buy my home and established myself in a good place in life. What I have learned is that I have more of my mother in me than I thought. I am strong and I wear my mother's shoes well, although they are not a perfect fit, I proudly adorn myself in her reputation.

She brags on me to some of my cousins, and tells them that I am doing fine and have grown into a responsible person. I thank God for my mother; she struggled to raise her family in spite of all of life challenges. She gave us so much of herself and because of her, I am Mary Jean the daughter of this woman called Mary.

When I needed help with my children, Mother was there with her knowledge, wisdom, and advice. I don't know what would have happened to my children if my mother had not loved us as much as she did.

The characteristic I love the most about my mother is her ability to adapt. My mother is a fighter and a survivor, and she never lets life get her down. I have never seen her at the point of hopelessness. No matter how bad the storm, no matter how darkness settles, my mother will survive. She says that God will not put any more on her than she can bare. I've seen my mother roll with some tough punches, and she always got back up. Don't get me wrong, my mother is flesh and blood like everyone else, but it is what she is made of that keeps her strong. Yes, she has cried, and yes, her heart has been broken. Yes, she has had a great deal of disappointments in her lifetime, but she has learned to adapt to all the changes in her life.

The most miraculous thing about her is that, in spite of all the pain she has had inside her, she has never become bitter. It seems to me that the fiery trials of life have made her come forth like pure gold, strong and refined. She never lets her personal feelings about a person interfere with that person's needs. She never stops giving and showing love. I have seen her go without, to help someone in need. My mother learned to adapt at an early age, because that was the only way she was able to survive.

One major characteristic I inherited from my mother is her courage. Courage is the quality of mind and spirit which enables one to faces difficulty, damage, or pain without fear. I say that courage is making the best decision in the most difficult times. It's like a soldier in a battle; you fight until the battle is won. I've seen that my mother was never afraid of life, and faced problems head-on. I saw her cry for the first time when I got pregnant, but she wasn't crying because she was afraid, but because her heart was broken. She prayed and cried out to God for courage to be strong, and to lead me during such an unsure time in my life. She got up the next morning with a new attitude.

She was strong and courageous, and ready for the next storm. No more tears; rather, she had a sense of direction, and a glow about her that wasn't there the day before. I have had my share of ups and downs, but I found the courage to go on. It took courage to fight to live when dying seem so much easier in the presence of desperate circumstances. It took courage to smile every day, even when I didn't want to. It took courage to believe in myself when it seems that no one else believed in me. I am not saying I am a saint, by a long shot, but by the grace of God, I had the courage to make changes in my life. It took courage to love myself beyond all my faults. I learned from my mother how to love the woman inside of me. She often told me, "Take care of yourself, and love yourself first before you love anyone else." Courage, and a blend or rare love has kept this family together for 40 years, and I have my mother to thank for that.

If I would give a part of my mother to my children for a keepsake, it would be her courage. If they have an ounce of her courage, then they will grow up to be happy and proud women. They would have the courage to discover that a woman is not the weaker sex, but the wiser sex, with a strong will to survive all odds and rise above the storms of life.

I don't know if I can be the kind of mother to my children

that my mother has been to me, but at least I have the courage to try. My mother's footprints are deeply merged in the sands of time. I don't believe that there is another human being like her on earth. Only her human frailty served to limit her courage from being unchangeable for this world.

If I had to tell the future grandchildren a bedtime story, it would be A Woman Called Mary. I would tell them about her amazing adaptability to changes, and how the story and history of old shaped her soul. I would tell about how one woman alone stood strong and tall against a cold, cold world, and raised ten children single handedly, and how she gave each one of her children a portion of her heart to carry throughout eternity. I would relate how she sometimes prayed all night, and taught her children how to love and to respect God. I would tell the grandchildren and the great grandchildren how she inspired her children to dream out loud, and to achieve the unachievable. When the world had lost all hope and courage to believe in human goodness, God sent them Mary. She is a hero to her children and to all who know her, for she is The Woman Called Mary.

Chapter 5
Lisa
Sister #4

My name is Lisa Thomas. I am the fourth oldest daughter of Mary Campbell Thomas DeWalt. Wow, that was a lot of names for one woman! Please bear with me as I attempt to enlighten you with my story of A Woman Called Mary. I would love to tell you all that my birth was well planned and celebrated by family and friends. The facts are there were already three little girls born before me, and it was a challenge being raised in a poor black household in the state of Mississippi. I grew up watching my mother struggle with things other people took for granted, such as having enough food for all of us on a daily basis. Don't misunderstand me; we never went hungry for long, because Mother always brought home food.

In the area that we resided, no one had running water inside of their houses or shacks. In order to give us all a bath, Mother would fetch water from outside and warm it up on the stove. Looking back on all of this makes me realize what a struggle my Mother went through in order to survive. I'm not sure if I could have survived back then, had I been an adult and endured all of the heartache and pain that she suffered.

My mother took us to the cotton field with her while she picked cotton. We would sat under a cool tree watching my mother pull a cotton sack that was twice her weight down the rows of fluffy white cotton. I watched the sweat roll down my mother's face as her cotton sack got heavier and heavier. When we all went home, mother would be so very tired, but she wouldn't say much, but just kept on moving—preparing dinner, washing dishes, preparing bath water, etc. The last thing she would do is make sure we all had clean clothing for the next day. I wondered how one person could work so hard and never complain.

I watched my mother make so many sacrifices for her children. I watched life hit my Mother with its most powerful punches, but she took them like a pro, and kept on rolling. Life gave her a beat down, and tried to make her surrender her life and her children's lives, but she was much too strong for that. I remember watching my mother cry, the tears flowed like rivers after a rainstorm, but as always after the storm, she would rise as the noonday sun, filled with power and glory. Sometimes I think that my mother walked through the fiery furnace of life and smiled at the devil, because she knew God had a better plan for her and all of her children. I often wondered, if Mother was not a woman who was familiar with grief and pain, would she still be the strong tower of faith that I have come to love and admire?

I vaguely remember the bus ride from Mississippi to East St. Louis. It was a long trip, and I was only six years old. I remember that when we first arrived here from the country, I had a difficult time adjusting to city life. I remember my first day of school. I had a mean teacher named Miss Griffin. She would hassle me about how to spell my name, because I was from Mississippi and spoke with a country twang that she couldn't understand. She had me to write my name as LISA

LEE that entire year. I'm not sure, but I guess it was spelled that way on my birth certificate. As I moved up to the third grade, I changed the spelling to how it is spelled today.

I always felt that I was the child that got little to no attention during my primary years. I was mostly viewed as the store girl. I was the youngest of the oldest set of kids, and the oldest of the youngest set of kids, which equals the invisible child.

One of the happiest days of my life was when Mother gave her life to GOD. I don't know why, but I always worried about her when she went to the nightclub with her friends. I remember always sitting on the side of my bed asking God to keep her safe and protect her. Don't ask me why; I was a serious-minded child who prayed a lot, and I still do.

I remember when I first got saved; I had to have been in the seventh grade. I don't remember how sincere I was about my religion, but Mother would always tell me about finding different friends to hang out with. My best friend at that time was popular with the boys. I really liked her, and thought that I could influence her to love herself so she wouldn't feel that she had to have sex with all those boys. I never did get her to understand how to love herself, and she didn't convert me over to being as popular as she was. Mother's thought was, "One would draw the other".

As a teen, I remember thinking that I had a miserable life, because all of my friends got to go to night clubs and school dances. The only place we got to go to was church every night, or every other night. But now, as an adult looking back on my upbringing, I wouldn't change it for anything. Truthfully, I wish I could give my daughter a piece of what my Mother gave us as kids. Because of mother, I am the person I am today.

When I was a sophomore in High School, I was dating this senior named Michael. Michael ran track and played basketball. I don't know how I thought I could maintain a relationship with him, when Mother wouldn't allow me to go to any of the dances, or go watch his track meets. Michael use to come over to the house to see me, and Mom would send my youngest sister Dena into the room with us, to watch us the entire time he was there. Eventually, he became smart and brought her some candy, or her favorite type of pickle, and she would get lost in her treats and fall asleep.

After high school, Michael went into the Army, but still kept in touch. He always call me, and even bought me this little promise ring. Oh, did I think I was in love! He wrote a few times asking me to ask my mother if I could fly to Hawaii to visit him. Mother, of course, said NO. Thank God she did, because Michael confided to me that if I had come to visit he wouldn't have sent me back home. Mother was strict, but a great mom—she was wheeling and dealing with her motherly instinct, and I am glad she was knowledgeable, and a great disciplinarian.

When I was in the 12th grade, for the life of me, I never applied to any university, or even thought of a career, because I actually thought that I was done. I thought I had obtained all of the schooling I needed, and I would now sit around and do nothing. This was my train of thought until my mother decided one day to ask me why I had not enrolled at Southern Illinois University. Boy, were my feelings hurt when she told me that I was either going to school, or going to work. So I, of course, chose school.

Even though my mother had ten children, she would always find a way to make each of us feel special. We all have our own special relationship with her, and it is sad to say but we are all spoiled and selfish about getting our time with her. When one of us is in need of help, Mother doesn't hesitate to rally the troops to help the one in need or in pain. My mother is special. I'm not sure if she realizes it or not, but she has a special gift. I always laugh and joke with Mom by saying "I know the doctors told you that you had ten healthy kids, but they lied."

Out of my seven sisters, I felt that I had the most fun growing up. My sister Jean was one of my best friends in High School, and we shared many things. As we got older, Mother finally started allowing us to go to different school functions. One Saturday night, Jean and I finally talked Mom into allowing us to go to a basketball game and dance together. The house rule was, "You leave together, and you come home together."

I have a lot of fun childhood memories, like when my mother decided to let my sister Jean and me go to the basketball game and dance. She specifically told us that we should come home together or we wouldn't be allowed to go again. We were so wild once we got from under Mother's thumb. When our curfew hour came I told my sister it was time to go and she looked at me and said "Girl, I'm going to get my whipping tonight, so you leave without me." So I did, and when I returned home, and Mother asked me where Jean was, I told her exactly what she had said. After Jean came home and got her whipping, she came upstairs laughing, and told me about how much fun she had. Those were fun times.

Out of all of the children, my sister Willie feels that my mother called me the strong one. I grew up to be the one she could depend on when things got tough, and she needed to talk through her thoughts. My mother would call me to talk to my other siblings when she couldn't talk some sense into them. I became the voice of reason for Mother. I think Mother called me the strong one because she sees part of herself revealed inside of me as her courage. I learned the lesson of courage by watching my mother's fearless strength during the storms of life. I like to think that each of us took something completely separate but worthwhile from my mother's personality. She gave us patience, courage, faith, hope, determination, long suffering, willingness to work hard, strong will, mercy, wisdom, and above all she gave us LOVE. Every time she looks at the ten of us, she sees ten different parts of her soul. We are the key to her strong will and determination to build a better life. We ten are the secrets that she and only she had hid in her soul, that not even time can erase.

I have a beautiful and bright daughter name Tina. I was so proud of her when she graduated from University of Arkansas in Fayetteville. I had many days while raising my daughter that I doubted my abilities as a parent, because I measured myself against my mother's parental skills. I am so proud to see that I didn't do too bad a job! One thing that I wished I could have incorporated into my daughter's life that my mother incorporated into mine was more church-going. As a youth I hated going to church all of the time, but as an adult, I realize it has given me a great foundation for life.

I believe my Mom is proud that all of her children have decent jobs. Thinking back around the first part of my chapter, where I described the struggles and the pains that Mother suffered to give us a better life, this is the point in the story where you can see it definitely paid off. I am pleased with both my personal and professional accomplishments. I never dreamed that I would be able to earn a college degree, and at this time I hold two degrees, a BA and an MBA! I owe it all to Mother for being the role model I needed as a strong Black woman. It forced me to declare at an early age what I wanted my piece of the pie to be, and to go and get it.

I would like to take my hat off to this Woman Called Mary, because she has demonstrated that strong will, determination, and a prayerful heart are the keys to surviving against the odds. My mother is the only person whom I have observed up close and personal, and I feel proud to say, "WELL DONE MOM!" You raised ten strong-willed children all by yourself, and you can look at each of us and see something that makes your heart proud. I hope that you feel as I do, that the struggle and pain that you went through in Mississippi was worth the reward you have received in the end.

I hope the story of your life will encourage some other young struggling mother with the determination that she can do it and put the fight back into their eyes. We as black people are known for long-suffering and fighting a good fight. We also need to be known as people that never give up, or give into life's obstacles.

Mother, I admire you because:

1. You're my Mom
2. You are a Black Queen
3. You have survived the lion's den.
4. You have grown stronger because of your struggles.
5. All ten of your children are productive members of society, and not incarcerated.
6. You are as beautiful inside as you are outside.
7. You made me who I am today.
8. You prove that one can rise above one's circumstances.
9. So many times, you bathed us with your tears, and clothed us with your love.
10. You proved that a good woman can raise a generation of productive children without the aid of a male role-model.

Chapter 6
Marla
Sister # 5

My name is Marla. I have two children—a son, Lawrence and a daughter, Raziya). I like to refer to myself as the centerpiece of the family, since I am the fifth of the ten. I'll begin to share with you my stories and memoirs as one of the descendants of the Woman Called Mary. During my childhood, my mom was protective of me. Being a child small in stature, I cried a lot and was always running to my mom for help.

My mom had a strong will, determination, and a made-up mind to overcome any obstacles that were blocking her path. As my mind began to take snapshots of my memoirs, the story began to slowly unravel. During the early 70's, when I was still young, I can recall that we were on government subsidies, and mother quickly realized that the monthly check she receive from the state couldn't feed ten children and her. I can also remember that when the last days of the month came, the cupboard would run low, but we always had food.

On check day, we would often be down to having only a loaf of bread in the breadbox and a bag of sugar in the cupboard. We made sugar sandwiches to eat for breakfast while mother caught a cab to cash her check and get groceries early that morning. When we saw the yellow cab pull up in front of the house, we all busted out the door screaming, shouting, and jumping for joy! This was just one of the many challenges that mom faced in attempting to raise her ten babies.

Not only was feeding ten children challenging, so was the task of clothing them. Again, mother started out on her journey to buy Easter outfits for each and every one of us. She soon had an eye-opening moment when she went into Sears and began her shopping adventure. She quickly realized that she could only buy clothes for half of her ten children. Anyone who knew Mary knew that this was not an acceptable solution. She was disappointed but began seeking alternative ways to clothe her ten babies. She immediately walked out of Sears and down the street to the fabric store. To her amazement, she found that she could purchase enough fabric to make dresses for all eight girls, and still have enough left to buy shirts and pants for the two boys from Sears. From that day forward, mother officially became a professional seamstress.

Growing up in the '80s as one of the Thomas' girls carried many expectations. In school, all the teachers knew you and your mom long before you were in their classes or grade levels. Once you screwed up, they didn't fail to call Mrs. Thomas. The first thing they would ask is, "You're one of those Thomas' girls, aren't you?" The teacher would go on to say, "You know your momma does not play."

I remember the sacrifices that Mother made in sending Lisa and me off to College in Carthage, Illinois. Financially, she couldn't afford for us to go, but she wanted us to have a good education and allowed us to go anyway. When I graduated from my 10-month secretarial program at Robert Morris, I decided that I would stay in Carthage for another six months to get my associate degree. My mom called up there to tell me that I needed to come home and get a job to help pay the bills. I didn't understand at the time that mother couldn't afford to continue to send money to me and Willie (who later came to Carthage), and support the other seven kids at home. As always, I adhered to my mother's demands and came home.

When mother came up in her station wagon to bring us back home, home wasn't home anymore. The house that we had grown up in was for sale. My mom, wanting to own her own home, bought a four -bedroom house, with a maid-house in the back. However, that house needed a lot of repair work done on it. The six kids and my mom stayed in the five-bedroom house while Jean and her daughter Kalishia stayed in the maid house. My oldest sister, Lillie, had already gotten married in the winter of 1979. The house needed so much work that we vowed never to tell our friends where we had moved. Mother kept saying, "It's mine, and it's paid for." Mother's determination never failed. She spent every extra dime that she came into on repairing the house. She didn't exactly know what the result would be, but she knew exactly what she wanted. With the help of grants, loans, and extra cash mother had, her shack became a home.

As the 80's spiraled out, mother finally begins to reap the fruits of her labor. She started to work outside the home as a seamstress at Levine Hat Company. Three of her daughters (me, Lillie, and Willie) were married. Lisa moved out. After I got married in '85, mother and I actually started becoming friends. Mother began to confide in me and valued my opinions. Life took another sweet turn when mother went out and purchased her first brand new car, 1986 Beretta Chevrolet, at the ripe age of 47.

I began my career at Southwestern Bell in 1984, and was making a decent salary. I allowed myself to reproduce the images in my mind of all the things that mom had denied herself in order to raise and educate her ten children. "We'll make the car fit into your budget; keep it, because you deserve it," we all told mother, and indeed she kept the car. Thinking back, I'm not sure who enjoyed the car more, my younger sister, Dena, or mother.

As momma's life began to blossom in almost every aspect of life, her heart continued to yearn for her family's unconditional love. Had it not been for the love experienced from her children, experiencing unconditional love may have never happened.

Thanks to momma, I have overcome all the stigmatism associated with young black children being raised by a single mother in the ghetto. The Woman Called Mary has proven the world wrong when they say that children are a product of their environment. I guess in a way it's true, for I am a product of my environment, in the sense that, like mother, I had to go out into the world and fight for my success. I am delighted to share with you that I am a black, middle age, educated woman working in Corporate America. By society's standards, I am classified as a successful, in middle-class family society. I have several credentials under my belt, which include two undergraduate degrees, one in Human Resources, and one in Information Systems. I have been employed at Southwestern Bell for 18 years, currently a web site designer in middle management. Self-motivation and self-determination created a strong-willed personality, similar to the one that mother displayed to us continuously. Because of her teaching, I was determined to succeed.

In January 2003, We moved into a brand new two-story home that we designed. My husband and I are also finding that we are making special provisions for our children, just as mother made provisions for me, to ensure that they too may obtain a quality education. I owe all my successes to my mom, who refused to let us settle for anything less.

Chapter 7
Velma Jean
Sister # 6

My mother Mary left the South at the tender age of 28. When asked why, she said, "I wanted a better life for my children." To her a better life meant a better future, which included educational opportunities for children. When she left the South, she left with expectations. She knew that many young lives depended upon her. She left Mississippi and boarded a bus, heading north, looking for better things. She brought eight girls and one boy with her to the big city. Though she was still officially married, her husband was gone so often, and had so little to do with the family, that she just as well have been single. Her strength, drive, and love for her children were her incentive. Upon leaving the South, we moved to East St. Louis, Illinois, which is where my mother's youngest child was born. Having many children was a lot to deal with, but God equipped her for the job.

We moved into a brick house on Columbia Street. It was a quiet neighborhood. In those days, your neighbors were your family, too. Everyone watched out for one another. My mother enrolled me in school, and I was so afraid that I ran away from school. Someone found me and took me home. I never did that again. Later, we moved again to Melody Lane in Park Side. There my mother enrolled me in John F. Kennedy Elementary School. By this time, I was more comfortable with myself and with going to school. My mother has always shown an interest in making sure we went to school. I remember an episode of her helping me with my homework. The subject was math. I had never been good with numbers. Math was hard for me to comprehend. My mother told me to, "Hold up ten fingers," but I held up eight. Finally, she said to me, "Hold up ten fingers, Velma!" I replied, "I don't have ten fingers, I have eight." She pointed to my hands and said, "What are those?" and I said, "Thumbs." Boy, did I get it that night! Technically, though, I was right.

When I was nine, we moved again. We relocated to north 14th Street. At that time, my mother enrolled me in Canady School, and things were looking up. My mother gave her life to God, and we became members of Colas Temple Church. My mother loved God, and she also taught us to love Him. We went to Church a lot, which is how we learned the value of a Christian relationship. Even though my mother was saved, we had a happy family life. I remember climbing trees, playing ball, and catching lightening bugs and grasshoppers. I also remember being the last one chosen for teams. Our neighbors were the Riches and the McKinney's. My best friend at school was my sister Myrtle, Thomas Benton, and Linnie Taylor (who was nicknamed Bayboo). Linnie and I met at school. Thomas lived down the street from us. The funniest thing about him was the bike he rode on. There were no tires on the bike, just rims.

Mom let us have so much fun, but we had to be inside the house when the streetlights were turned on. My mother made sure we were clean. The older siblings had to bathe the younger ones. My mother had a lot on her plate, but her pride was in her children. She made our clothes, cooked our meals, and made sure our hair looked nice. Our birthdays and Christmas Days were always the best. On those days we would run down the stairs in the morning, because we knew that my mother had some special gifts for us. After passing from the 6th grade, my mother enrolled me at Rock Jr. High School, which is where I met Rita, who became my best friend. We are still best friends to this day. Upon graduating from Rock, I went to East St. Louis Senior High. Once again we moved; this time my mother bought a house in Washington Park. It was in the early 80's. My mother worked, and she sent us to school.

Mom was always determined that we would go to school. She used to tell us, "You may not be going to school, but you are leaving here, and if I call the school, you'd better be there." In 1983 I graduated from high school. The ceremony was held at the Shrine of Our Lady of The Snow. My mother and my siblings were there too. They cheered us when we marched for our diploma. My mother's hard work, efforts, prayers, and determination had paid off.

Even as a child, I remember my mother asking me, "What would you like to be when you grow up?" After graduating from High School, my mother took me to enroll in College. I enrolled in SIU-Edwardsville, and went there for just one semester. At that time I was not ready for college, but I was only going because it was the right thing to do, or so I thought it was at the time. I left SIU after that one term, and in 1985 I enrolled in Capital City Business College, where I earned a Certificate as a Nurse's Assistant. In 1986, I attended Mildred Louise Business College, and later received a Certificate in Secretarial Studies.

In 1990 I gave birth to a son, Damian Young. At that time I lived at home with my mother, who helped me to take care of my son. My mother raised us well. She had done a good job that, by the time I reached the dating age, she knew I was deserving of her trust. She had taught me morals and values, to have respect, and to do what was right. She also taught me and my siblings to always let someone know where you are. Even though my mother is strong, she has a sensitive side as well. I remember her telling me, "When children are young, they are on your hands, but when they grow up, they are on your heart." I have never forgotten those words. I keep them in my heart. I really love my mother who has been a significant influence in my life, and in my heart.

My mother is a well-rounded person. Her qualities surpass those of any woman. She can paint, hang drywall, sew clothes, change the oil, cook, clean, sell, and count better than most people. She definitely has the ability to be an accountant. God equipped my mother with so many splendid talents. However, the most important thing He has given her is the gift of salvation. In fact, she raised us in righteousness. I remember when Christ started dealing with me. I talked to my mother and she prayed for me and even though she had prayed all my life, that night, God saved me and I received the Holy Ghost.

Because of the values my mother instilled in me, I am able to instill those principles in my son. Principles such as loving God, having respect, being honest, loving others, having integrity and goals, were lessons I taught to my son. My mother has always been an honest, loving person. She taught by precepts and examples. She worked an honest job. She respects herself as well as others, and believes that people should work for the things that they want. She also believes that the family which prays together will stay together. I thank God that my mother has always prayed protections upon our lives. Having nine siblings is a lot to contend with, but our family is blessed, because we love each other.

On holidays and weekends we come together and have fun. I could not imagine my life without any of my siblings. Today, I work as an Educational Counselor Assistant, I teach Sunday School, and I am a college student pursuing a degree in education. If it was not for my mother's help, I would not be able to go to college. She keeps my son when I take an evening class. Not only that, but she picks him up from school, because I work full time. Because of the values and principles, my mother has instilled in me, I strive for excellence.

There is so much that can be said about The Woman Called Mary, but I believe Proverbs 31 describes her, especially when Solomon proposes the question, "Who can find a virtuous woman?" Proverbs 31:10: "For her price is far above rubies". Proverbs 31:13: "She seeks wool and flax, and works willingly with her hands. She is like the merchant ships; she brings her food from afar." Proverbs 31:15: "She rises also while it is yet night, and gives meat to her household, and a portion to her maidens." Proverbs 31:16b: "With the fruit of her hands she plants a vineyard." Proverbs 31:17: "She gives her loins strength, and strengthens her arms." Proverbs 31:18: "She perceives that her merchandise is good." Proverbs 31:19: "She lays her hands to the spindle, and her hands hold the distaff." Proverbs 31:20: "She stretches out her hands to the poor; yea, she reaches out her hands to the needy." Prov. 31:21-31: "She is not afraid of the snow for her household, for all her household are clothed with scarlet. She maketh herself coverings of tapestry; her clothing is silk and purple. She maketh fine linen and sells it. Strength and honor are her clothing, and she shall rejoice in time to come. She opens her mouth with wisdom, and in her tongue is the law of kindness. She looked well to the ways of her household, and eats not the bread of idleness. Her children rise up and call her blessed. Many daughters have done virtuously, but thou excellest them all. A woman that feareth the Lord shall be praised. Give her of the fruit of her hands, and let her own words praise her in the gates."

Those scripture describe her best. Life has not always been easy for her. I have seen her struggle, but even in her struggles, she has always been blessed, and optimistic, too. "I have never seen the righteous forsaken." (Psalm 37:25b) My mother is truly a mother at heart. Now I understand what she meant when she said, "When children are young, they are in your hands, but when they grow up, they are in your heart." I realize that, no matter how old your children get, they are still children to you, and you never want to see them hurt or suffer.

Although my mother is a serious person, she also makes me laugh. An incident happened once when one of my sisters was lost in another city [Memphis, TN], and called home for help. Although my mother did not know how to find my sister, she said, "Just stand in the middle of the street, because I am coming to get you." Fortunately, the situation was resolved and my sister was located, and my mom did not have to go to Memphis, but I know she would have. To me that just signifies the depth of a mother's love.

One of my funniest memories was when my sister, Dena made herself a sandwich, and left the kitchen only to return to half a sandwich. I had eaten the other half. She told my mother, but my mother never said a word, because she knew that was something that siblings do to each other.

The other thing that strikes me about my mother is her devotion. My aunt Rose had been sick for a long time, but my mother resolved to be there for her. No matter how tired my mother was in her own body, she would always put my aunt and the needs of others first. I would go by mother's house to pick up my son, and my mother would be so tired you could just see the exhaustion on her face. I would suggest that she go and get some rest, and she would say, "No, I have to go see Rose, and I am going to church after that." Sometimes she wouldn't have time to eat until 11:30 at night, because she put the needs of others first. Yes, this tells the story of the unselfish, unyielding love of A Woman Called Mary.

Recently, my aunt passed. She went on to glory, but on this side of the earth she will be missed. Although, I know my mother misses her, she truly put her time in. I told one of my sisters, "The one thing about it is, no one could ever say that my mother was not there for my aunt. I have seen my mother in her dedication to my aunt. Her love for her motivated her to go see her, cook, pray, and stand by her. Yes, these are the awesome qualities of my mother, A Woman called Mary. God gave me to my mother thirty-eight years ago, and I am so glad that God does not make mistakes. He gives the right children to the right parents. Though mother was and is a single parent, she has done a tremendous job raising us, and some of her grandchildren. Smile.

My mother is one of the best-dressed people I know. She can out shine the finest. Her style is classy and unique. She loves clothes, shoes, and purses that match. She loves to shop, and she takes pride in how she looks. I remember an occasion when I wore this suit which, because I had lost some weight, was now too big for me. My mother looked at me and said, "I really wish you would not wear that suit until I can take it up." It was funny, yet it showed the depth of my mother's love. I think she still saw me as her six-year-old child.

In this moment, I still wonder how my mother raised us all. She did so well that even Mother Teresa would have taken notice. There is no one else like my mother, A Woman Called Mary. Now that I am grown, I can understand some of what my mother went through. Even though times were tough, God gave her the strength to raise her children. Because of her, we are all productive members of society. Today my mother is still a strong, dedicated, loving, independent person, who speaks her mind.

My mother was not overly protective when I was growing up; she gave us room to grow. Growing up in a big family, you always had somewhere to go. My sisters are funny and loving women. Along with their personal success, they have also become successful parents. They all are stunningly beautiful, but they are very easy to approach, and grounded. Normally when people meet others of such high intelligence they are intimidated, but my sisters are easy to talk to. My brothers are kind-hearted, yet bold. They have fine qualities about themselves as well. We are all working people. The qualities that we have came from our mother, A Woman Called Mary. A good seed produces good fruit. Children are the reward of the Lord, and blessed is the man, or in this case, the woman, whose quiver is full of them.

I have a suggestion for everyone who reads this book—always love your mother, and listen to her, because mothers always know best! No matter how old children get, children never get as old as their parents. That is why the Bible says, "The older women should teach the younger ones." Wisdom is the principle thing, and wisdom comes with age and experience, not just from books. To my mother, who is the significant influence in my life, I bid you God's best, and I know his blessing is and always has been upon your life. You have done an outstanding job, and I want to say, "Thank you for raising me. Thank you for putting the needs of your children first. Thank you for my church upbringing. Thank you for taking care of me when I was sick. Thank you for enforcing education in my life. Thank you for teaching me to have a great work ethic. Thank you for your hard work, wisdom, love, time, and effort. You have planted godly principles in me. A Woman Called Mary fits you appropriately. May the Lord bless and keep you, Mother. You are the best in this plight of life." In conclusion, I want to thank God for my siblings, and, above all, I praise God for my mother, A Woman Called Mary, who was, is, and always will be a significant influence in my life. Love—Velma.

Chapter 8
Myrtle Steen
Sister #7

In Loving memory of my husband,
Pastor Rueben Shannon

My name is Myrtle Steen. I am the seventh child of Mary. I am married to Ruben Shannon and I have two boys, Lamondez Thomas, and Jerry W. Dewalt Jr.

My mother has a way of making all of us feel special. She makes me feel special when she calls me to discuss the Bible or the Sunday School lesson. She values my opinion on things, and I love that. She and I often go shopping together, because she admires my tastes in fashion.

From the beginning, mother often placed the needs of her children above her own safety and comfort; she always wanted the best for her children. I inherited her fierce independence that carries a great cost, a cost that can never be taken lightly, or for granted. Over the years from childhood to adulthood, I was shaped by her sacrifice and her strength. She will always be my Superwoman.

My mother is a warrior, a soldier, and a nurse to her children. Even if it meant neglecting herself, she provided in every aspect for us. Her love can conquer anything. It is a love that sees only the best in you, and a love that is real and everlasting.

My mother has flair in dressing and putting together colors and designs. I inherited my flair in dressing from her. I love clothes and shoes, short haircuts and bold colors. People say I look like my mother, and I'm proud to know that, because she is a beautiful woman. My mother takes pride in her appearance. "There will never be another you, so make sure you leave a lasting impression." My mother meant that!

I will try to be honest about my life, and how I see my mother Mary. She is indeed a wonderful woman. God established her going and her coming. He tried her in the fires of life, and she came forth as pure gold. She reminds me of the story of Job in the Bible in how she had patience in her suffering after losing her mother and father at a young age. She held on through the struggles, the tears, and even the heart aches, and she continued to stand on the word of God. No matter how dark the nights became, and how long the days were, she waited until her appointed time. You see, God makes and molds us. He carves the soul out of the circumstances we survive in life. Through her suffering, my mother began building faith, courage, determination, longsuffering, meekness, kindness, and, most of all, love.

My mother is always saying that, "God is a good God," no matter what comes her way. I have seen her bending like a young green tree when the storms of life blow, and still standing strong when they stop. I began to see the emotional, spiritual, and physical toll that being our everything was taking on her. She gave all she had to her children, even if looked at times like we weren't going to make it, but with the help of God, she brought us out all right. That is what I call strong determination in her faith.

I watched my mother, when she brought her first message. My heart rejoiced inside my soul, as she went forth speaking about the Acceptable Fast. She never liked to talk in front of people, but now God has exalted her to new heights; and she was great in teaching people the word. She was happy to please the Lord by teaching how to present one's body as living sacrifice, holy and acceptable unto God, undefiled by the world. Watching her speak to the people brought joy to me, because she was happy.

She spoke out of her soul and with knowledge. Her life is full of testimonies. Our hearts were glad as we feasted on the word of the Lord. As she spoke, my thoughts were, "Who better to speak the living word of God but The Woman Called Mary. Powerful and anointed is what this woman is."

I am an Evangelist, Missionary, and a Pastor's wife. I am faithful and dedicated to the Lord, to my church, and most of all to my husband. Because of my mother's prayers, and the life she lived, I am a better person. I wanted to serve God like my mother. When you asked children what they want to do when they grow up, a few will say, "I want to be like my mother." Today I'll tell the world that I wanted to be like my mother, I want to walk in her footsteps. I wanted to serve God like she did, and to stand strong on my convictions like she does. I wanted to live a saved and sanctified life as she does. She is my mentor, and my anchor in God. She was an example of faith because she showed faith in every part of her life. She believed God would make a way even when we could not see a way. Sometimes I thought she was crazy for believing when things looked hopeless. All mother had to lean on was God, and she believed beyond a shadow of a doubt that God would work it out. She believed that God would keep food on the table, and He did. She believed that God would keep a roof over our heads, and He did. She believed that God would make away for her to pay the bills, and He did. She believed that God would heal us when we were sick, and He did. She believed that God was going to teach her how to drive, and give her a car, and He did. I never saw this kind of faith used before, but she showed me how it worked.

We went to church at least three nights a week, and twice on Sundays. My mother kept us on the altar, and in the prayer line. She anointed our heads with so much oil that we smelled like olive oil. My whole life began to revolve around the church, and that is where my heart is today. I always wondered if those three angels, Surely, Goodness, and Mercy were still hanging around the state of Illinois.

I will never forget that I was told I was born with a veil over my face, meaning I had a spiritual gift to see beyond this world. I did not understand why I could see ghosts or spirits, but I could. Once I saw a man walking beside me and no one else could see him. He didn't bother me, he just kept walking, but he scared me to death. Sometimes I know things before they happen. This is not a gift I wanted to develop, but one that I wish would go away. I am still trying to figure out why I have a gift I didn't want. I have more fear of this gift than I have comfort from it. I often talk to my mother about it, and she always says, "Pray about it, and let God guide you." She always has a positive way of looking at things, and a way of making you feel all right after talking with her. She understands the trouble I see and the agony I have about being able to see things not of this world. She comforts my soul when I am mentally distressed.

My mother is a hard worker, and that is another trait I inherited from her. Mother did not have money to buy us dresses, so she made them herself. She would sit at the sewing machine for hours making clothes for us. On Sundays, we would all step out dressed-to-kill. Mother was the best seamstress around. People paid her to make their clothes. There were ten of us, but every Sunday we were all dressed for the best.

Even though we were raised on a one-parent income, we were clean and well fed. We didn't look like the poorest kids on the block, even though we sometimes were. When God is in the plan, little becomes much. Like my mother, I am a hard worker. I got my first job at age 13, working after school at a daycare center, helping with the children. My next job was at the age of 15, as a bagger at a grocery store. I have been working ever since, and my biggest desire was to have my own business. My family would always laugh at me because I would always find something to sell, from candy, to fish, chicken dinners, accessories, purses, and clothes.

One day my dream came true. I opened a business called Myrtle's Accessories & Things. I give God and my mother all the glory, because she instilled in us the attitude that we can be anything we want to be, as long as we put our heart into it. Mother taught all her girls to be independent, and take care of themselves, and not be dependent upon on anyone else. I think we were all trained well to be independent. We all watched my mother struggle to raise ten children, and we were determined to not give up, for a winner never quits, and a quitter never wins.

My mother taught us that being black is not an excuse to fail, but a reason to excel. Being an independent, strong black woman doesn't always go over well with everyone. Some people see us as bossy, because we all have a sense of direction about us, and a well-developed sense of integrity and pride in ourselves. We realized that we have no control over life and its situations. However, if you happen to be a child of Mary's, then you know better than to lie down and die over a little bit of bad luck.

She taught us to be strong and rise to the challenge, and give it your best shot. We all know how it feels to not have anything, and yet be happy. It takes more than a little bad luck to make one of Mary's children depressed. Don't get me wrong; we are still human, but we had a great motivator and wonderful example of courage in adverse situations.

We are blessed to have known the power of prayer, and we learned that, as long as Jesus is sitting on the throne there is hope, because prayer changes things.

My mother prayed all the time. Sometimes you could see her lips moving, and other times you could hear her pray out loud. There is something beautiful about hearing my mother calling on the name of Jesus when she didn't know what to do. It put the fear of God in me, and it let me know God is real. I am so glad that I learned how to pray at an early age. I learned that we are not alone in our problems and despair, because God is there to strengthen us in the time of need.

The bad thing about so many children today is that no one in their homes prays, and children don't get that close-up and personal experience with God from their parents. Prayer will keep a family together. We learned to pray together as a family. We all got on our knees and prayed as a way of worship, and as a nightly way to thank God for watching over us.

It is so sad that today praying is almost outlawed in our society. Loss of prayer is the gain of pain in today's families. If prayer was placed back into its rightful place in society, then there would be fewer suicides and drug overdoses, and less prostitution and murder. People perish because they think there is no hope, but there is hope in the love of God. There is hope in having a personal relationship with God. People are looking for hope and love in all the wrong places.

I was blessed that my mother introduced me to Jesus, and showed me how valuable he should be in our lives. I am grateful that my mother cared enough to share her faith with me. I am doing the same thing with my children, telling them about Jesus, and how He can change their lives and work out difficult problems. I want my two sons to trust in Jesus when all hope is gone, and to know that when they can't talk to me about things, then they can talk to Jesus, and He will never let them down.

Family is important to my mother, and she loves to have all of her children visit at one time. I admit it; we all spoil her now, because the Bible says, "Her children shall grow up and call her blessed." She loves the holidays, because we all gather in one house to give thanks, have dinner, conversation and to reflect on our blessings. We all cook and bring a covered dish, so that no one person is over-worked, and we share love and family.

My mother has this proud look on her face, as she looks around at all her children and grandchildren. It feels so wonderful to belong to a large, love-filled family. I am overwhelmed with tender tears of silence when I think how God has blessed all ten of us to be healthy and prosperous. The way we all love and respect each other is amazing to me. We always find a way to help each other achieve their dreams. We are there for each other, and we love being together. I am sure that this is what God had in mind when he invented family. It is because of my mother's love that we have learned to love each other. She instilled in us that we are all that each other has, and one day she will not be here, and that we should always love and respect each other.

Education is also important to my family. Most of us have post-secondary degrees and certificates. My sister Marla was the first one to graduate from college, earning a BA in Computer Science. In addition, Lisa has a BA in Business Management and a Masters in Advertising. Willie has a BA in Health Care Management and a Masters' in Business Administration. She also has so many other talents and skills. She and I both write poetry; she has even been published in two books. Willie, being tall and thin, modeled for ten years or more. She writes her own music, and has released one CD, and is working on her second. She is also writing a book of poetry.

Rickie has a BA in Business Management and an MBA. He

is so smart, and we are all so proud of him. Velma is in college working on her degree in psychology. She has a 4.0 GPA. Dena has a certificate from a business school, and works at Southwestern Bell as a supervisor. Lillie has a certificate in Secretarial Science and is a professional secretary. I went to Belleville Area College to further my education. I received a certificate in computers at Bits and Bytes computer school. I write poems, and I wrote my first song, called I'm Going All the Way, which my sister Willie has included on one of her CD's.

I plan to go back to school to further my education in Business Management. I am currently working at The St. Louis Job Corp Center, counseling and mentoring students who have decided to make a new start in life. My job is to help motivate them to become whatever they want to be in life, and to teach them that there is nothing too hard, if they put their heart, soul and mind in it. With teaching that, success sits around the corner. "If you believe it, you can achieve it," I say to them. Most importantly, we can do all things through Christ who strengthens us. My sister Jean is working a 9-to-5 job, and Lee has always been a hard worker. I will not end this without thanking God for my wonderful sons and our beautiful grandchildren. Last, and not least, to God be the glory for my loving husband, Pastor Ruben Shannon, who has been a great supporter and inspiration in my life. I just want to say, "Thanks, 'Bae.' I will always love you."

My heart overflows with emotions as I end my story about The Woman Called Mary. This is certainly my reality, that she did an outstanding job raising ten children. Her strength and determination carried us through some hard times, and

Mom, I want you to know than I'm proud of you. It is a blessing to be able to say that the main character in this book is my MOTHER. I give ridiculous praise of gratitude to this beautiful woman. I love you, Mom, and to God be the Glory!

Chapter 9
Dena
Sister #8

My name is Dena. I am the youngest girl. I have a son André Philip. I grew up in the mid-1980s, in East St. Louis, IL. I was about one year old when my mother moved to Illinois. Because I was so young I had no idea of the struggles my mother was going through at that time to raise the ten of us. I heard horrible stories from my older sisters about how hard it was being raised in Mississippi. Some of the things my mother lived through seem unreal, and sometimes I wonder if my physical make-up is composed of the same genes as my mother's.

One reason I wonder this is because I cringe a little every time I think of what she lived through. I don't think I could have done it. I can't tell you about the night we escaped from the nightmare in Mississippi on a slow bus ride to East St. Louis, Illinois. I can't tell you about the tears and heartaches my mother battled in this thing called life, but I can tell you about her life and her struggles after we got to East St. Louis.

I will walk you through my life with my mother as I watched her hair fade from black to gray. I was there through thick and thin. I am the youngest daughter; I am an attachment of her soul. I am the mirror that reflects the story of hidden pain and untiring love of this Woman Called Mary. I witnessed her bathing us in the tears of her struggles, caressing us in love, prayer, and her blue yonder mountains of faith. When my sisters were growing up all around me and leaving the nest, I was still there. I saw her life at its worst, and at its best. I have no poetic words that can pour rivers of emotion into the reader's soul. I am not a profound writer of elegant memoirs, or of publicized, well-written novels. What I am is the last daughter of A Woman Called Mary, who wants to persuade readers to find courage and strength to deal with a life of heartache and pain through her struggles. I can't tell the world why the caged bird sings. What I will tell the world is how joy was so abundant in her life, even though it was filled with disappointments.

I grew up with many older siblings, and watched my mother get all of them up every day, and get them dressed and ready for school. I couldn't wait until the time I could go to school. I wanted so desperately to go. They seemed so grown up, and all I could do was grab their books when they came home from school and look through them. Finally, it was my turn to go! I was in pre-school at John F. Kennedy. My sisters would walk me to school, and then they would go to King Jr. High School. I was so excited about school that I didn't sleep at all the night before the first day. I was finally a big girl! I went to school all excited for about a week. The next week the teacher announced we were going to the clinic tomorrow. That day my sisters walked me to school, and as soon as they left me, I went back home and stood in the back yard hanging around the house waiting for school to let out. After about 20 minutes of hiding, my mother was in the kitchen making coffee, and she saw me standing in the backyard. She came to the door and asked what was I doing, and why was I out of school. I lied and said we got out early. Being the mother that she was, she asked why there weren't any other children walking home. I really thought she would be angry with me. Mother called up to the school and learned that we were going to the clinic that day. Once she got off the phone, I thought I was going to get the punishment of a lifetime. To my amazement, mother simply asked them to not take me to the clinic when they go, and that she would take me herself.

To most people this may seem to be a small thing, but the courage of mother standing in and making everything all right was a small example of her making sacrifices to keep her family safe. This made the difference in my enjoying school in my later years. From that point on, I loved school. I never wanted to miss a day of school after that. As soon as I was old enough to go to the same school as some of my older sisters, it seemed they were always about to graduate. When I finally made it to the first grade, my sisters Jean and Lisa were in the sixth grade. My sister Jean use to be a patrol girl, and she would come to my room and pick me up every day so she could walk me home.

That next year Jean and Lisa were not there, but my sisters from Marla on down were there, so I still felt comfortable. I was always good in school. My sisters or my mother would never have to spend time with me to help me with my homework, and I was always a focused child. Mother did not have to spend a lot of time developing me, because I was never there to cause her any worry. Of course, my sisters will not let me forget that when I was around two, and my brother Ricky was the baby, I would always take his bottle from him. That's what they say; I don't remember it myself. Maybe I wasn't ready to give up the bottle yet!

Growing up with a big family means you always have a playmate. My mother would never let us spend the night at our friends' houses. She would always say, "It's enough of you all to have your own," and that's what we did. We would have our own baseball team, but as soon as the neighborhood kids saw our Gang out there playing, they all joined in. I remember my sister Marla would always get up when it was her turn to bat, and she would have her famous saying, "You can depend on me," and would strike out each and every time.

I remember once when my mother went down south to Mississippi to visit my great Aunt Lillie, and she left my sister Lillie in charge. This was the first time my mother had left us. We had to beg Lillie to go outside and play, but we couldn't get outside of the fence. We cheered inside the fence, and before you knew it, all the neighborhood kids were standing outside the fence watching us. Lillie came to the door, saw us, and made us come in the house. She was not having that! We tried to explain we weren't doing anything. She made us come in and get in our own separate corners in the house, and sit there. That was a horrible weekend. That was the first and the last time she kept us for the weekend.

I was so glad to see my mother when she returned. I was jumping up and down and screaming. You would have thought I had won a million dollars! From that point on, she would take us with her when she went out of town. Every year, my mother started taking us to Mississippi to visit my Great Aunt Lillie, and we would stay for two long weeks. That has been our family vacation every single year. I remember it being the summer of the fifth grade and we were in Mississippi visiting Aunt Lillie and we were walking across the railroad tracks to the store and I ran into Tracy Glass, a boy who was in my class back in East St. Louis. I will never forget that. It turned out that His grandmother lived three doors down from my Aunt. I remember him calling my name, and I looked, and it was him. Talking about the world being a small place; we both were there at the same time, hundreds of miles from home!

The summer of 1981, Aunt Birdie B.'s house burned down, and she decided to move back to Mississippi. I rode down with her, and was waiting for my family to arrive two weeks later, and I called my mother to see when they would be arriving. She said she was not coming down that year. I was so upset, because I knew I didn't want to be there without my family. I called my mother every day, crying. I even told her I was going to walk home. My mother was trying to catch a bus down there to get me.

Aunt Lillie would not let me hangout with Aunt Birdie, because she didn't want me running the streets. So I hung out with Aunt Lillie, and she would take me back and forth to church with her & Aunt Mae, which seemed like every night. We would go and visit my Aunt Mae, and I would at least get to play with her daughter Jackie. We would ride her ten-speed bike with no tires on it. It was scary, but Jackie thought it was great. My mother had sent me a whole box of clothes, ones she had made, of course, which made me the best dressed girl there at the church in Mississippi. After two weeks of Mississippi, they called and told my aunt Birdie that her insurance check had come from her house burning down. She said she was going to get it and would be back, and I couldn't go because I would try to stay at home with mom. I begged her to let me go, and finally she said, "Okay." I sneaked all of my clothes out of the back door to the trunk of her car. After about two hours of driving, Birdie said, "I saw you sneaking your clothes out to the car." All I could do was laugh, because I was going home. I had never been away from my mother before, and that was long enough!

We finally stopped going to Mississippi every summer, and that was cool with me. I started to hate it down there. I vowed I never wanted to go again. My sisters were off in college, and traveling became too expensive. I returned home and was entering the 10th grade, which was exciting for me. I was finally growing up! I enjoyed going to East Saint Louis Sr. High School. I had two sisters, Myrtle and Velma, attending there. Of course, they were senior's, and I was a sophomore, which was cool with me. No one believed I was their little sister, because Myrtle was wild and Velma was so quiet. I was in between both of them. Myrtle's boyfriend would chase me thru the halls every day. I hated him for that.

I loved school, and I would never miss a day, until the time this skank girl, named Twanna, wanted to fight me, because she said I thought I was cute. My mother had to come up to school. My sisters Jean and Lisa would always get into fights. Mr. Lewis, the principal, use to call me Hollywood. When my mother arrived, he said, "Hollywood, I know that is not your Mother, because she doesn't play." He had gotten to know her well with all my sisters who came before me. Just like him, anyone who knew my mother knew she didn't play.

I graduated from East St. Louis Sr. High in 1985, when

Ronald Reagan was President of the United States. The world was unsure of what tomorrow would bring with Reagan in the White House. To most black people he was a ticking time bomb, which could set black people back about 15 years. His shinny dark hair added an air of fear to the oddly aged-shaped face. In black neighborhoods all over the world, they called him the devil, or the mark of the beast.

Black people lived in fear, wondering what horror was awaiting them at the hands of President Ronald Reagan. I can remember my mother praying for the White House, asking God to lead the President, to help him make good decisions. I was too busy being a teenager to worry about President Reagan. I was the youngest girl in the house, and my mother had become soft and melted down, saying "yes" more than "no."

Yes, I was happy, but like the rest of my sisters, I still didn't get a chance to date until I was 17; that was one rule she stuck to. I did get to go to dances and football games and be a part of the pom-pom team. One thing that I regretted and was angry about was my high school graduation. The night of my graduation no one showed up to cheer me on. I was disappointed and devastated that none of my family was there to cheer me on for such a special day. I know there is no such thing as a perfect mother, so I still give my mother two thumbs-up for making the effort to be the best.

For the first time of my life, I was not the focus of my mother's attention. There was something far more urgent than me. Three of my sisters were away at college. Myrtle and Velma were riding with my mother, who had to be somewhere else.

I know that my mother could not be in two places at once, but at that moment, I wished she was there with me. I am not selfish, I just wanted the one person who struggled with me and raised me for 17 years to share in my glory.

I admired my mother, because she had a loud wonderful laugh that invited others to laugh with her. My mother found pleasure in mothering. As we were growing up, mother didn't have the money to dress all ten of us, so she prayed to the Lord to teach her how to sew. Mother used to sit up all night making clothes, from dresses to pants to slips. She would make the prettiest ruffled dresses and hair bows. We may have been poor, but we were the best-dressed family at the church.

Living under her roof, you were going to church, and you were going to be a participant in whatever church activities that were going on. The good thing about Sundays was all the young people would hang out at our house after church because they knew mother would be serving her famous Sunday dinner—greens, smoked neck bones, and cornbread with chocolate cake, roast beef, and potatoes.

Mother wanted to give us the life she never had, a life filled with love, and someone who cared. Between the prayers, and those three angels: Surely, Goodness, and Mercy, we were well-protected, and well-rounded children. My mother always gave good advice, and she seemed to know everything. My mother may have started out with a limited education, but she could add faster than the cash register. When she went to the grocery store, she added the food as she bought it. She always knew when the cashier was off a couple of dollars.

There was never a shortage of love from mother. You would think that with ten children, all different in personalities, we would have felt less love at times. Nope, Mother treated us all the same, but she responded to our situations based on level of importance. Yes, the problem child at that particular moment in time got her attention, but she never forgot about the less needy children in the family, and she was always full of support, and had a listening ear of love. She was never too busy to give advice, even when you didn't want it. She would always remind us of the saying, "I have been where you are trying to go," meaning, listen to me; I can give you good solid advice.

It was nice when all my sisters had finally moved out of the house; I used to drive mother's cars all the time. I would drop her off at work and pick her up. It was good. I was the last girl, finally. I would go to the hairdresser every two weeks, and get to do some of the things my sisters could not do. Finally I moved out, went to college, had my own apartment, and was living life as mother had taught me to do so. Well, not like she taught me, because I met a man, fell in love, and became pregnant. The baby's father wanted me to marry him, but I didn't really think he was the one. Mother saw me and asked if I was pregnant. I admitted it, and we talked afterwards. She gave me the best advice a mother could give, saying, "Just because you made one mistake doesn't mean you have to make two." That summer of 1991, my mother received that great awful call that Aunt Lillie had passed. I was seven months pregnant and we packed up for that final trip to Green Wood, Mississippi. The hot Mississippi sun, burned so much, I felt hot and sick every few minutes. It was sad; the only mother figure my mother had in her life was gone, and the only grandmother figure we had in our lives was no more.

We returned home to Illinois, and our lives resumed. My son was born Sept 6, 1991. Mother asked one last time, "Are you sure you don't want to marry him?" I replied, "I'm sure, and the answer is still no." I knew at that point that I would be okay. I know that I would not have made it thus far if it was not for my mother. Whenever I got lifted up in the pride of my joy and face, my mother would let me know. Life blinds the young with ignorance, but a wise woman builds her home one brick at a time in the days of her youth, and when she is old peace and security will follow her.

This may sound stupid to someone outside of the family, but the situation paved a road to great achievement and better life-making decisions. She kept my son while I worked and went out to clubs and everywhere else. She had him so much my sisters would call him my mother's last son. Being a grown woman and having my mother still there for me was a true blessing. I love and thank her for it to this day. My sisters and brothers are still close to this day, any time you come to my mother's house you will find at least five of us at my mother's house on any given Saturday, just to be there. We are still that same close family as we were growing up. Still, to this day, we've got each other's backs!

My cousin Rosie Mae died November 5, 2002, at the age of 65. My mother was there praying and making intercession in prayer for Rosie Mae, night and day. My sisters Willie and Lisa were telling my mother to prepare to let her go, because she was not going to live through this. My mother was brokenhearted and troubled for her cousin. You see, they were raised together like sisters, and they shared a life bond.

My mother could not let go no matter what her children said. I watched my mother, with mingled gray hair and golden-bronzed complexion, smile and say, "I miss talking to her." Mother really didn't want to let her go, because she was a big part of her small circle of love, and now it would be broken again. I could look at my mother's face and see that death had cheated her so much in life, that now she wanted to fight death for the precious life of her cousin Rosie Mae. My mother stood there as Rosie Mae called out to God in agony, "Lord, how much worst is the pain going to get?" My mother's heart dropped. She realized then that it was time to let her sweet cousin go.

Rosie Mae had a kidney transplant, and it worked for about four years, and then things began to deteriorate. My mother walked with a slight rock to the left as she walked over to the bed to comfort Rose. Her dark deep eyes filled with tears, her voiced trembled, and she began to pray with Rose. Rose looked up at my mother as if she could feel my mother letting her go. Death had already filled the room. Rose face took on a more peaceful profile and her grip on my mother's hand loosened. The look on my mother's face was one that words could not describe and could not explain. It was lost between great sorrows, peaceful relief, and feeling cheated again by death. My mother needed us, and most of us were there for her. We wanted to do so much more than watch her suffer the pain of losing Rosie. We wanted to bear the pain and loss for her. For once in life, we wanted to stand in the gap for her in this dreadful situation. I know it isn't possible to bear another person's load; we humans can only make the load feel lighter by giving love and support.

My friends used to always tease me and say, "Dena, we are not coming to your house, because you have the meanest mother in the world!" I thank God for the meanest mother in the world. I am now 35 years old, and have lived this life with my mother to guide me through. With her prayers and her determination, I am a strong, young, black, confident young woman. If she could raise ten children being young, black, and single, surely I could raise one son with the same strong will, determination, confidence, and faith that my mother instilled in me.

Mother, I love you; you mean the world to me. If I can be half the woman that you are, I will be blessed. I take my hat off to you, The Woman Called Mary, because you are some kind of wonder for all of us.

Chapter 10

Rickie
First Son

I am Rickie, the ninth child of Mary, whom you may know by now as The Woman Called Mary. I am her first-born son, the one who will carry on the family name.

I was born in a day and time when my people were fighting for equality, and dying in the process. It was a day in time in American history that travailed with the pain of giving birth to part of Martin Luther King's dream. I arrived just in time to witness the bloodstains on the hands of America. America the Beautiful was forced to repent for her mistreatment of black people. Without a heart she sucked the life out of her young black sons and raped her black daughters. I thank God and all the people who helped America give birth to a safe delivery of change.

My life had a rough start, but God gave me strength to live on. My mother was twenty-seven years old when I was born. She already had eight little girls, who were more than ten handfuls. When I came along I brought with me sleepless nights and heartaches for the whole house. I was a preemie. Mother delivered me two months early, and back in 1968, Mississippi was not prepared to be accommodating to a premature black baby boy. I weighed less than three pounds, and was sent home in an incubator to test the will of God. If it was not for the love of my mother, I would have died. We had a fat-belly wood-burning stove that heated the entire house. One of the conditions of my survival was that the temperature had to remain the same. A drop in the temperature meant I could possibly die. My mother was a tower of faith, and she believed that my life would go beyond the incubator. The six months following my birth were for my mother times of exhaustion and, at times, sleeplessness. She watched and prayed over me many nights. I gave her a few scares along the way, but nothing that her love could not handle.

Every time my struggle to survive demanded that she give more, fight harder and love more, she answered without complaining. Surprisingly, Mother still managed to take care of the other eight little girls, in spite of me being so demanding of her attention. She must have taken care of them as I slept because when my eyes opened she was there. I grew up in the will of God and the love of my mother.

My mother didn't have servants to help with the children, cook the food, clean the house, bathe the children, or wash the clothes—she did it all by herself.

A mother's love is more powerful than any other force on earth. Nothing can compete with a mother's love. My mother was rich in love. It was like a well of love flowing from her soul, bathing all in her presence with the purest love the earth could hold. I am so blessed to have her as my mother. As I write, my eyes are welling with tears, because I know it was love, and only love, that gave my mother the courage to be courageous in the midst of this difficult situation. I dare to think that if she slept too long one night, or if I had caught a cold, I would not be here to tell you about my beautiful mother, Mary.

My life hung in limbo for six months. For six months, Death took a seat in our house, waiting on me to take my last breath. Mother wrestled with Death for six months, night and day, eventually robbing him of his victory. I stand here today healthy, holy, and blessed. Because of my life this Bible verse is so dear to me "Grave, where is your victory "Death, where is your sting" 1 Cor 15:55 (KJV) For anyone to lay down his or her life for another is something powerful. The best gift I have received from my mother is her love. Yes we were dirt poor, but rich in love. We survived Mississippi surrounded by love.

Let us examine the word love. I looked it up in many dictionaries, and some of the definitions were, "profoundly tender, passionate affection for another, feeling warm and deep personal attachment, having affection, and concern for the well-being of others," and finally, "to have a strong liking to." I was disappointed in the definitions the dictionaries provided.

These words will never do when talking about the love my mother had for her children. My definition of my mother is 1: Love is the force that bridges the road between life and death. 2: She guards the wall that protects her ten children. 3: Having the courage to live, instead of dying in the midst of hardship. 4: To nourish, protect, and prepare a young black man to survive in a white man's world. I am sure everyone have their own definition of love, but there are times when the words of others won't serve the purpose.

My mother taught me how to be a man. She molded my outlook on women and family. She had the courage to stand up and show the same strength that a man would show if he were present in the home. She was both mother and father. She had the wisdom and the courage to raise a black male child into a grown, productive man. When society and statistics state that black males raised without a father in the home became trouble for society, I laugh. I disagree wholeheartedly, because during the era of slavery black women were the ones who raised the boys into men. If all things in the world were equal, we would find that white boys would get into just as much trouble as black boys. The trouble and issues in which they face are different, but the growing pains are the same.

My mother's biggest fear after we started growing into teenagers was losing one of her children to the streets, or to the bullet of a white racist police officer. We grew up on the cold facts of racism and what being born black in America truly meant to a black male. Mother told us that the world will hate you for no reason other than that you are black. She said, "The weak hate because they lack the courage to love; but in the end, it's their problem, not yours."

You should always rise above hate with love. Fools will hate without a reason, and teach their children to be fools, because it takes courage and intelligent to love. My mother told us how to handle racist police officers when stopped for walking in the wrong neighborhood, or for DWB [Driving While Black]. My mother said it's better to live to fight another day than to die at the hands of a white man. The courage to love in all circumstances is better than hate.

My mother kept us away from drugs by introducing us to

God at an early age. Mother's religious upbringing was not in vain. We kept it all in our hearts. Lord knows we went to church every time the church doors opened. That is one reason we stayed out of trouble as teenagers. There were plenty of good, positive, strong black men in church, and they spent time with the young men. I admired my Pastor, Elder King J. Tyrus. He was a really good man, and a great friend. I loved to hear him preach the word of God. I regret that Elder Tyrus died before I reached adulthood. He and my mother shaped my outlook on life.

If I had to say one thing about my mother, it would be that she is truly amazing. Never is she too busy to listen to our problems and give advice about handling life's mishaps. I guess the fire burning in her soul gave her the courage to be strong when the forces of this world fought against her. I watched my mother rise to the challenge each day.

What part of my mother's personality did I receive? I

think I have received my mother's quest for knowledge. I've built my life on gathering more and more knowledge, to help my people overcome the stigma of being black in America. In my eyes, there is nothing more beautiful than an educated black man, who can take care of his family. My mother taught me that knowledge is power. With power, we can conqueror all things. Seeking knowledge grants you the power to change. This power can change your communities and your world today, yesterday, and forever. Mother, you are my hero. You made me the man that I am today, and today I say, "Thank you" a million times over!

Chapter 11

Lee
Second Son

In loving memory to our dear brother

My name is Lee Arthur Thomas. I am the youngest of ten children. Growing up in a family of eight girls was hard; no man should have to endure that kind of agony! I love my sisters, but they were extremely bossy. Thank God, there were two bathrooms, because one was always filled with girly stuff. I really don't know how I turned out to be so manly; let's just say I adjusted quite well.

Within my thirty-six years of life, I have been married twice. I guess I was looking for a woman like my mother—strong, hardworking, sweet, and possessed of a strong sense of family. Both marriages came with pre-existing conditions, and they failed to make it on the applications. It turned out that my first wife didn't want children. It would have been nice to know that before we sealed it with a kiss at the altar. My second wife, who was twice my age, had sons that were close to my age. I am sure you have guessed by now that both marriages were disastrous.

Despite two failures, I still desired to be married and raise a family, but I am determined that this next time I would take my time looking, to ensure that I have found the woman I wanted. Mother had told me not to marry both of the first two; she said I was rushing into the marriages. She was right;

waiting, and getting to know them, would have saved me much heartache. I'm loosely quoting this, but he that findeth a wife findeth a good thing. Well, that remained to be seen. My second wife tried to kill me by running over me. Seeing me dead versus being with another woman suited her well. I think she thought she was providing me with tough love; but in reality, I loved that woman, she was beautiful! With the first wife, we got married at eighteen, and Lord knows that was too young. She and I lived with my mother for three years, until we got on our feet. Being married at her young age wasn't about the happiness of love; it was about getting away from home. For some strange reason I had a bad habit of rescuing women in despair. I guess that knight-in-shining-black-armor thing should have stayed in the movies. I am a romantic at heart. Being happily married and serving as a deacon at church; pleased me fine. Nevertheless, life has not allowed me to settle down with that perfect wife yet. I have learned a lot from both of my wives. Lessons learned and forward I moved.

After I left both marriages, my mother sat me down and had a long talk. She made me look at myself, to examine why I was attracted to a certain type of woman. What was it I needed from them? She let me know that I had to find out who I was before I could truly be happy. I think because my mother raised us alone, I developed a need to rescue women who had trouble finding their way in life. My mother was a troubled woman, but she was strong, and found her own way in the world. I guess somehow in my sub-conscience, I felt as if I was my mother, who did everything possible to rescue and save her children from harm and despair. My mother's spirit is all about helping, teaching, and saving. The problem was, I was interpreting things wrongly, and it cost me dearly.

Being the youngest in the house molded me into being the needy one. I didn't want to be left out. I wanted to be used and appreciated. Even standing six feet seven, I am a man with a heart of gold. I wanted validation in all of my relationships.

My biggest problem with women was when they complained about a problem they created. They complained, and it got on my nerves, but the fixer in me tried to make things right. I never understood why my wives got mad with me when I told them how to handle their problems. I thought the reason they were telling me the problem was so I would do something about it and make them happy. In talking with my mother, she explained how women want men to listen—not talk, not solve—just listen. Mother explained how women are not helpless, but they simply want to vent, to release their tension and move forward. "She is not helpless," Mother told me, "but she feels better to get it out, so just listen."

I was told women like for a man to take control and make all the decisions. But then when I did, we would always get into fights about me being too controlling. Women, they drove me crazy! I did the best I could to keep the bills paid and food on the table, and every now and then gifts of love, but I still couldn't make them happy. The more I did to build a home the more they did to tear it down. My mother made me realize the women I had chosen had far more problems than just being married. They had issues that they should have dealt with before marriage. Until they got rid of those old ghosts they would never be happy. My mother helped me to see that my attempts to rescue troubled women can be hard on the heart and mind. I tried hard to make these marriages work, and it broke my heart to watch myself fail twice as a husband.

My mother raised me and my brother Rickie well. She taught us how to be men, and how to respect women. She gave us good values to build our lives on. She said, "Don't date anyone you would not want to marry, and stay away from them easy girls." She always told us not to take advantage of the ladies, and to remember—no means no. If you take the girl out, then be a man and bring her back home at a decent time. Don't sit outside in your car blowing your horn for her to come out; go in and meet her parents. She said that if our hormones can't be controlled, then protect ourselves, but it is best to abstain from premarital sex. "Don't bring no baby home before you take vows."

I heard on a talk show once that a woman can't raise a male child. I strongly disagree with that. My mother did a wonderful job raising her two boys. She taught us how to stand strong.

Gang violence is one of the biggest problems for black males. Most kids join gangs because they experience for the first time male bonding, whether good or bad. Some of the kids in gangs do not have fathers at home, and are forced to join. They are forced to join because they are told that if they don't, their family members will be hurt or killed. Therefore, out of fear, and wanting to protect family members, good kids go bad.

No kid is going to confess to his father that he must join a gang, or the family will suffer violence. Out of concerned for family, they reluctantly join the gang. I don't have answers for how to cut down on gang activities. I thank God for my mother's protective spirit. If there are no black fathers in the home, I pray that black mothers fight harder to save their sons from the gangs. Mothers, talk to your sons. They need role models or big brothers; they can find some in the churches, the schools, and the community centers. Mothers, you owe your sons a better solution than joining a gang just to find male bonding.

We were raised in a poverty-stricken town, but my mother stood strong. She was the wall that fenced us in from the destruction of the world. Don't get me wrong, the gangs, such as the Disciples and the Bloods, chased me home every day, trying to force me to join them. They caught me once or twice and beat me up. My mother called the police, but they did nothing, because they didn't know where to find these boys. I didn't give any names. I told my mother not to call the police again, and that I would be all right. No matter what they did, I was determined not to join. My mother kept me in the prayer line, and stayed on her knees asking God to intercede on my behalf. God worked it out to where one teacher saw me running home one day and noticed about fifty boys chasing me. She stopped, picked me up, and drove me home. My mother picked me up for a while, and then my teacher started letting me out of school 30 minutes early, so I could get home before the gang boys were out. My mother was there offering support, and encouraging me to be strong and stand, because help was on the way; God would deliver me. Finally the gang lost interest and stopped chasing me. God worked it out.

My brother and I grew up without selling drugs, joining a gang, or earning a prison record. Mother is my hero, because she made me the man that I am. I am not ashamed that a woman raised a male child into manhood. I am strong with pride and dignity; I am not suffering from a male deficiency disease because there was no man in my life. Don't get me wrong, having a good father around to help raise me would only have improved my life. Unfortunately, destiny had other plans, and they didn't include a man in my life. My mother was both mother and father for us for over twenty years. I have a strong sense of manhood and an even greater sense of my blackness.

Momma had strong rules, and we were to always obey them. We had 30 minutes to get home after school. If we were late, my mother came looking for us, and she didn't have a second thought about embarrassing us in front of our friends. She had a reputation for hunting down her children; and it only happened once to each of us. After that one time, believe me, you didn't want her to come after you again! Don't get me wrong, if you had been previously asked to do something after school, and she knew about it, then she would let you do it, but we were never to do anything like that without her permission.

I remember once when I started to grow like crazy and at 6ft, 5in, I made the mistake of talking back to my mother. She knocked the air out of me so fast, all I remember is getting up from the floor. She is a 5 ft. 5 superwoman who hits like Mike Tyson. I would never want to get into a fight with my mother. I learned that day that she didn't care what size you were, when she said do something, you did it, quickly, and without any back-talk.

My sisters always complained that my mother spoiled us

boys, because we were on the end, and the girls cooked our food, and washed and ironed our clothing. After the girls were gone, mother began to mold us boys into self-sufficient men. We can cook better than most women. We can wash and iron as well as a woman, and clean house better than most women. She taught us how to work with our hands to make a living, as well as using our heads. She taught us the role we play in the family as a man. I will always remember my mother telling us to live up to our responsibilities like a man. She told us, "If you sleep with that woman and get her pregnant, then you owe the child your life. If you don't want to marry her, then pay child support and be a part of the child's life."

My brother Rickie is a great father to his four children. He has a college degree, and works two jobs to take care of all four children. He is a police officer, and he works in a business job at Southwestern Bell Phone Company. He and his wife are both in church, and they are raising their family by their Christian values. It is wonderful to see this in a day and time when everything you read is talking about the absent black fathers. I think there are more black fathers staying in touch to help raise their children than back in the 80s. Black men are starting to step up to the plate and be men. With so much going against us as black men, we realize that we need to be a part of our children lives, to keep them strong. Churches are teaching us to honor our responsibility, be good fathers to our children, and the best husbands we can be to our wives.

I was recently reading an article that asked the question "Are Black Father's Necessary?" What kind of question is that?

Let's get real; the black family's troubles have always exist in this country. It started with slavery. Frequently masters would sell off the black man from his family, and breed his wife with other male slave, to get more slaves. They separated the family and broke down family barrier to keep the men away from his wives. The next thing that was done was government welfare programs. Welfare rewarded the mothers, and made them chose between food for her child to eat and having the father in the home. Welfare would not give a poor black mother support if the father was in the home, which made it easy for him to walk away for the good of the child.

We all know how hard it was fifty years ago for a black man to get a job. If he had no job, how could he raise his family with pride and dignity? The black families of old have been done a great injustice. There was so much effort given to tearing the black family apart in America society, and some of it we men did with our own two hands. The government should put forth the same amount of effort in putting the black family back together again. Unlike Humpty Dumpty, it is possible to put us back together. We can, and will, reunite as a strong family fixture in America. I think a full pledge campaign should be launched to putting the black family back together. I would like to see in my life time commercials and movies made which promote positive images of black families. There should be a grant for black couples who graduate from college and marry each other. There should be scholarships for black husbands and wives to complete school. I read that my prayers are being answered, and that encouraging black families to stay together is a high priority with Federal, state, and local governments.

The article I read was called, "Turning the Corner on Absentee Fathers in Black America." It had positive potentials for putting the black family back together. The problem is that this project has been in operation since June 16, 1999, and I am still waiting to see the effects of it. I haven't heard anything about it, but it reads well on paper. Reality is another story altogether for black families. They even got Morehouse College involved in rounding up deadbeat black dads. Morehouse has encouraged Civil Rights organizations to move this to the top of their agenda.

Now it seems that the failure of the black family is under a microscope for all to examine. I think the answer is simple— instead of putting the mother and child on welfare, give the father a scholarship, so he can learn what he needs to find a good job, or start a business. The price of a four-year scholarship is a lot cheaper than 18 years of welfare. It is a true saying, "Give a man a fish and he eats for a day, but teach a man to fish and he can feed his family." I hope it is not another empty promise made by Congress to get black people's juices flowing and get free votes.

The statistics are astounding; an estimated 80% of all black children live in fatherless homes. This is evidence that the black man has never been able to shed the slave mentality when it comes to being a father. He still thinks as a slave; get the woman pregnant, make the master happy, and walk away. Black men are their own worst enemies, because there is power in the family structure. The family is a vital part of a productive society. Rome fell with the destruction of the family unit, and so did the black family.

I would like to say that I thank God for my mother. When I look at all the young black men I grew up with, I am even more grateful for my beautiful mother. She was strong and firm with my brother and me. We complained that she was to strict, and that we could not even breath without her examining the air around us, but if there were more mothers like her, the jails would not be so full of young black men. The drug dealers would not be selling drugs in the black community, because there would be no one to buy them.

I admire my mother because she is full of wisdom and knowledge. I don't know how one woman can be so smart and full of love. If she had not loved the ten of us as much as she did, where would we be? I was the last one born, and I am sure the choice of having another mouth to feed didn't exactly make her heart thrill. Me being a man, if it was me and I found out that I was pregnant for the tenth time, I would break down and cry. I would have cried because of the situation having to raise another child alone.

The world is not perfect, and sometimes society can make pregnant women's lives seem hopeless. They scare the pregnant woman, and then say, "We can help ease that load at the nearest abortion clinic." I am so glad that the most trying time of my mother life proved to be a time when she chose love. She chose love; she had to love her unborn child enough to give the gift of life. I smile every day that I look at my mother and I feel a deep emotional feeling of thanks. I sometime walk up to my sweet mother and say thank you for loving me. I am a 6 ft, 7 inches tall man, but my mother's love reduces me to tears of warm laughter in my soul when I think of the bitter road she traveled. No greater love has a mother for her son than to lay down her life and take a chance on love. The greatest gift a mother can give her child is the gift of life.

After months of thinking about this decisive moment, I have decided not to go into that good night without telling and saying one last good bye. You see, I did marry again for the third time. My search for the perfect wife and two twin girls has brought me here in March 2012; to a place where I am fighting for my life. I am dying. At the close of my life I see things so differently now.

I see absolute truth. I see broken dreams and lost hopes, yet I feel the glory of God. I see crystal rainbows and yonder skies over a magical mansion of promise resting on purple colored mountaintops. I am dying and yes, I see the dawning of a new day. God gave me two beautiful twin girls, and I love them with my whole heart. If I could have requested a few more years it would have been spent loving my daughters, but heaven only knows. With God's help, I have forgiven the person who murdered me. But I will not deal with that right now, because my days are few and my mind and heart are more focused on sharing my mother's story.

I just want to thank my Pastor and First Lady Elder Loren W. and Lillie Burris, and Mother Cora Belt, along with the Foundation of Truth Church for all their prayers and love. With that being said I must use my last breath to finish my mother's story because there are three angels in my room now.

No mother should ever have to bury her child. There is nothing I can do to stop this day; death is coming like a runaway train. At least my soul has found peace with the fact that I must leave this world. I cannot bargain with death for more time, because my time was appointed at my birth. I watched my mother press her way to the hospital every day for two months to see me. I would look up and see in her eyes so many questions that only God can answer. She was on a walker and crippled by a much needed knee replacement, but though her body was riddled with pain, it did not stop her from making her way there to my bedside every day.

I was an eyewitness to the deepest love a mother could have for her child. I felt it in her spirit, and read it in her eyes that, if she could, she would give anything to exchange places with me. This is the only time I have ever seen my mother helpless but wanting to do more than her human body could do to bear this cross for me. Mother always had answers for me, and knew how to fix and heal our aches and bruises, but now all she could do was cover me with her love.

So she bathes me in her tears, and clothes me with her prayers, and I have been comforted. The person I am going to miss the most is my mother. I am praying that I can take all my memories with me as I go into my next life. Mother, I will soon be in God's hands, and He will heal me through death. So don't cry any more tears, and don't remember me sick. Remember me full of life, standing full of the glory of God. Mother your job of loving and taking care of me is done, and was well done. I would not change a thing about the time I shared with you.

To all my sisters I say, "I love you all, and take care of momma; her heart is broken, but in time it will heal." To my big brother Rickie I say, "You are the man of the family now. Take care of everyone in the family. I love you man." To my mother I say, "Mother, now you are facing your biggest test of faith trust and love. This test of love is letting me go and trusting your faith to carry you through the hardest and deepest part of human frailty, death. Don't fight for me anymore; use your strength to hold the family together. Mother, like Mary, the mother of Jesus, standing at the foot of the cross, burdened with sorrows, and battling with everything within her soul to see the bigger picture, I need you to see that God's will is being done in my life. He gave you a son to prepare to meet this day, and I thank you for teaching me how to pray, and for living a good Christian life in front of me. Thank you for teaching me that, while death is an unwelcome part of our lives, it is a necessary transition to eternity. In sorrow, this thing can tear apart the entire planet, but you can minimize the damage caused by death in our family by standing strong when it would be so easy to fall down under this kind of pressure. Mother I am asking you to "stand," and when you have done all you can do to stand, you stand anyway, because standing strong is what you do."

Momma, with my deepest gratitude I say, "Thank you for loving me. I will be waiting for you in that place where time is no more and there is no more pain, no more worry, and every day will be Sunday, and the streets are paved with gold." This was a job well done by a wonderful Woman Called Mary.

PS!! I am sending you love from me and those three angels, Surely, Goodness, and Mercy, who watched over us all these years, they are here with me now. Momma good-bye for now, I know we will meet again. Remember, heaven knows! I will always love you.

Minister Lee A. Thomas

www.ingramcontent.com/pod-product-compliance
Lightning Source LLC
LaVergne TN
LVHW020055090426
835513LV00029B/1629